Conversations with

JEAN PIAGET

Translated by Basia Miller Gulati

Jean-Claude Bringuier

Conversations with

JEAN PIAGET

The University of Chicago Press
Chicago and London

Jean-Claude Bringuier is a French journalist and
television interviewer. In addition to Piaget, he has
interviewed Albert Schweitzer, Gaston Bachelard, Indira
Gandhi, Edward Teller, and F. von Weisecker, among
others. In 1962 he was awarded the Prix des Critiques
for his television film *Cinq Anglais pour Noël.*

The original French edition of this work appeared
under the title *Conversations libres avec Jean Piaget,*
copyright © Editions Robert Laffont, S. A., 1977.

The University of Chicago Press, Chicago 60637
The University of Chicago Press, Ltd., London

© 1980 by The University of Chicago
All rights reserved. Originally published 1980
Midway Reprint edition 1989
Printed in the United States of America

Library of Congress Cataloging in Publication Data

Bringuier, Jean-Claude.
  Conversations with Jean Piaget.

  Translation of Conversations libres avec Jean Piaget.
  1. Cognition in children.   2. Intellect.
3. Knowledge, Theory of.   4. Piaget, Jean, 1896–
1. Piaget, Jean, 1896–   II. Title.
BF723.C5B6513   155.4'13'0924   79-15669
ISBN 0-226-07505-2

Contents

Foreword to the English Edition

Conversations with Jean Piaget by Jean-Claude Bringuier, translated by Basia Miler Gulati, is a most interesting, refreshing, and stimulating book. It offers far more insight into Piaget the man, scholar, and teacher than any other book available. We see Piaget simultaneously deep and light, serious and joking, presenting himself as he really is, playing with his cats, smoking his pipe, and being quite open and candid. We observe his personal and professional impact as well as the manner in which he works as an epistemologist.

Jean-Claude Bringuier successfully presents a comprehensive and articulate interview on the intricate subject matter of Piaget and the Geneva School. In order to grasp the importance of this book, it may be useful to say that it was elaborated in conjunction with a French television series for which Piaget had agreed to be filmed discussing not only academic but personal topics. The result is a real portrait of Piaget and his School, and, because the first group of interviews was conducted in 1969 and the second not until 1975, we can observe the essential continuity that exists in Geneva. In 1975, for instance, Jean-Claude Bringuier finds Piaget even more strongly committed to some ideas than he had been in 1969. In brief, *Conversations with Jean Piaget* offers, among other things, an opportunity to understand his development over time.

Finally, let me say that during the twenty years or so that I have known Piaget, first as a teacher, later as a colleague and a friend, one aspect of his personality has always struck me greatly: Piaget writes the way he thinks. This is what makes him difficult to read and understand. In *Conversations with Jean Piaget*, because of Bringuier's remarkable ability and sensitivity as an interviewer, we are offered a rare opportunity to overcome these difficulties. The translation, moreover, is excellent.

Gilbert Voyat

Foreword

We have refrained from a strict editing of these conversations; apart from some tidying up to make them easier to read, scarcely any changes have been made. The meaning and value of our project lies in their very spontaneity. The man whose conception and development of his life's work have been unfolding for more than half a century bears witness to it today; his view of it is given from the perspective of the moment in which we question him.

We hope to show Piaget as a whole and yet in the present, with the transformations of viewpoint, the omissions, and the obsessions of one who lives his work. It seems to us that this principle faithfully reflects the spirit of Jean Piaget, who has characteristically reassembled the gains of his past research and introduced them into the work in progress, and has done so with a stubbornness to match their depth and age, from the studies in botany, zoology, and his first works on behavior in the human animal to the subject that now concerns him: an account, at once descriptive and theoretical, of the development of the human mind.

The reader will forgive the clumsiness or naïveté with which some, perhaps the majority, of the questions are expressed. We have chosen not to hide them or correct them after the fact, thinking their very awkwardness may encourage the reader, if he is unfamiliar with the field or scarcely more familiar with it than we ourselves were at the beginning, to follow these informal conversations, which sometimes are overly commonplace and at other times, when we were unable to lead Jean Piaget to a further simplification of ideas, a little too sophisticated.

J.-C. B.

Preface

Jean Piaget is both famous and little known.
A great many people know vaguely that a scholar by that name
lives near Geneva and that his work, based on interviews with
children, is of major importance. In the Swiss capital they recognize the silhouette of the tall, slightly stooped man, with his
ever-present beret and white hair; they also recognize the ancient
bicycle, which even yesterday carried him to the Faculty of Sciences from his suburban house and takes him every Saturday,
regardless of the weather, to the nearby mountains for a long
ride.

His collaborators revere, not the psychologist of childhood,
but the philosopher of science who has chosen the child as an
instrument of knowledge; the biologist who as early as 1920 had
grasped the basic intuitions of cybernetics as practiced today in
every research center; the epistemologist whose annual seminars
draw scientists from every country and every discipline.

The image that greets the visitor who meets him at home for
the first time is picturesque and misleading: the image of the sol-
itary scholar, in the style of Pasteur, that we have inherited from
the nineteenth century. Imagine a square room with daylight

entering through two windows that overlook the garden. Standing in heaps around the high-backed leather armchair, stacked against the walls, gently spilling across the table and even stuffed beneath it, are piles of books, file folders, and notes—hills and mountains of paper. In this immobile tumult can be glimpsed a teapot, a mug, a can of tobacco, some old hats faded by the mountain air, and, somewhat incongruously, a telephone.

Translator's Note

Piaget's technical terms, though kept to a minimum in the present work, present special problems of translation which require for their solution the expertise of a Piagetian scholar. I have been fortunate in this respect to have close at hand Terrance A. Brown, M.D., of the Illinois State Psychiatric Institute. I am indebted to Dr. Brown for his clarification of many terms and passages and for other helpful suggestions that have contributed much to the readability of the translation.

Basia M. Gulati

First Conversation

What is Psychology?
(May–June 1969)

> *As I enter, he swings the armchair, where he has been writing, around to face me.*

Jean-Claude Bringuier: Please continue if you have something to finish.

> *(Piaget smiles and takes off his glasses.)*

Jean Piaget: Not at all. It's better to stop in the middle of a sentence. Then you don't waste time starting up. When I write, I always stop in the middle of a paragraph. The great advantage of writing a book is that it lasts for a year or two, whereas, when you write a letter, you have to set an entirely new process in motion.

> *(I look around at the mountains of paper and piled-up folders that fill the room.)*

Bringuier: You have a funny office—one rarely sees one like it. I'm tempted to say it's a mess.

Piaget: As you know, Bergson pointed out that there is no such thing as disorder but rather two sorts of order, geometric and living. Mine is clearly living. The folders I need are within reach, in the order of the frequency with which I use them.

Bringuier: Still, to find a reference from ten or fifteen years ago under all this . . .

Piaget: True, it gets tricky to locate a folder in the lower levels. But if you have to find it, you look for it. That takes less time than putting them away every day.

Bringuier: But when the house is cleaned . . .

Piaget: No one cleans here!

Bringuier: Never?

Piaget: Never!

Bringuier: How does your wife . . .

Piaget: She's kind enough not to touch anything.

> *(He fills his pipe for the first time. During the beginning of our conversation, the housecat has come in by the open door and settled itself under its master's hand, which dangles from the arm of the chair.)*

Piaget: Here, kitty.

Bringuier: It's not very obedient.

Piaget: It's uncertain.

Bringuier: What's its name?

Piaget: "Cat"! Why name it?

Bringuier: When you call "Cat," it comes?

Piaget: Oh, no. *(Leaning toward the cat.)* Here, kitty! "Here" it doesn't understand very well, but it understands "No." When it shouldn't come in, you just say "No."

Bringuier: Is it a real companion or a sort of plaything?

Piaget: It's a nice cat. Everybody loves it. People fight over its company.

Bringuier: Do you let it in when you're working?

Piaget: Of course. Not on my lap but beside me. Here, kitty.

Bringuier: There's a little of everything in here—insects in glass cases on the walls and plants at the windows. At what level of life does psychology begin, do you think?

Piaget: I am convinced that there is no sort of boundary between the living and the mental or between the biological and the psychological. From the moment an organism takes account of a previous experience and adapts to a new situation, that very much resembles psychology.

Bringuier: For instance, when sunflowers turn toward the sun, that's psychology?

(He smiles, hesitates, then nods.)

Piaget: I think, in fact, it is behavior.

Bringuier: Isn't there any boundary between sunflowers and us?

Piaget: No. That is the central argument of my book *Biology and Knowledge,* in which I try to show the isomorphisms . . .

Bringuier: The analogies?

Piaget: Yes—between organic regulations and cognitive processes, the processes of knowledge. There are structures of organisms and structures of intelligence. I try to show that the latter spring from the former and that logic, for example, originates in the general coordination of actions and that the general coordination of actions is based on coordinations of the nervous system, themselves supported by organic coordinations.

Bringuier: If sunflowers act "psychologically," can one go even lower in the living world? How far down?

Piaget: How far? The question arises when you see films like the ones the biologist Paul Weiss has made, showing the cell's internal movements. Paul Weiss has good cause to say that the language of behavior is the most suitable for explaining such phenomena. It expresses the facts better than a purely physico-chemical language. So if "behavior" is found even within a cell, this increases enormously the scale of behavior and thus of psychology, which is not the science of consciousness only but of behavior in general.

Bringuier: Of conduct.

Piaget: Of conduct. "De la conduite," as my professor, Janet, used to say.

The living organism is capable of foreseeing, of anticipating. In the world of life there are all sorts of anticipations. You mentioned the plants, which in fact I am studying; the bud, for instance, prefigures the flower, just as the stages of embryogenesis prefigure full-grown organs, and so forth.

I wanted to study a case of anticipation that would show much greater variability and would allow a detailed analysis, species by species.

These plants, the sedums, lose their secondary branches, which fall to the ground and make new plants; the fall is prepared for, the fissures shrink, and so forth. For any given species there is a series of anticipations, a series that varies greatly from one environment to another. All this among living things that have no nervous system. No brain. This interested me, and I studied it. You see only some of the plants here, the most delicate ones, which have to be protected. I have others growing in the garden.

Bringuier: But aren't such anticipations blind? I mean, do they "know" they are anticipations?

Piaget: We don't know anything about the possibility of consciousness in plants.

Bringuier: You don't believe in it?

Piaget: Well, I don't know anything about it! We don't know anything about animals' consciousness either, yet we can believe in it. We don't know when consciousness begins for a baby or a fetus. It isn't a problem. *(He sees my astonishment.)* It's true! Psychology isn't a science of consciousness; it's a science of behavior. We study behavior, including consciousness when we can; but, when we can't, it isn't a problem.

Bringuier: You are saying that psychology begins when something reveals psychology?

Piaget: When the organism behaves with regard to external situations and solves problems. From the moment such problem-solving isn't programmed by heredity, as instinct is, it's a psychology that closely resembles human psychology.

The case of instinct is a specialized animal psychology, a subject like any other.

(Kitty, "the cat without a name," has managed to curl up in Piaget's lap and is purring.)

Bringuier: Where does consciousness begin in the animal kingdom?

Piaget: Ah, that's insoluble; there is no criterion. I imagine there are degrees of consciousness at every level—but only degrees. One can have consciousness of an act and not integrate it; I call that elementary consciousness. For example, I am absolutely not visual. When I'm out walking, I pull out my watch and sometimes say the time out loud, or I whisper it. If I say what time it is and recall the sound of my voice, I can remember the time. If I say nothing, and it's purely visual . . .

Bringuier: You forget!

Piaget: A minute later I pull my watch out again, and then I realize it's still the same time. I was conscious the first time, but I completely forgot: it wasn't integrated. I must have been conscious of it when I looked at my watch, but, by failing to integrate it, my consciousness disappeared when I stopped looking. If I say something like "five after two," then I can remember it.[1]

Bringuier: But in the ordinary sense of the word, consciousness means knowing one has consciousness.

Piaget: No, that's already refined.

Bringuier: It's the usual meaning we give to the word "consciousness."

Piaget: It's already an upper level of consciousness.

Bringuier: A level reserved for man?

Piaget: I don't think so.

---

1. Piaget's watch, like his beret, is famous. It came to him from his grandfather, a watchmaker. He is never without it, carrying it in his sweater pocket on the end of a chain and consulting it conspicuously, at conferences or lectures, whenever the speaker wanders. He is always on time, that is, early, for work sessions and appointments, for trains and planes. When he flies, he habitually sits close to the exit in order to be the first to leave. He explains this set of idiosyncrasies by saying, "I was born three weeks late and haven't ever made it up." In fact, the real time that causes him to hurry is that of the work to be completed, the work in progress, the work incessant.

Bringuier: For chimpanzees?
Piaget: I imagine!

> *(A silence. Piaget and I smoke our pipes. Kitty is sleeping.)*

Bringuier: If I say, "I have a blue and yellow notebook," I will never know whether you see the same blue and the same yellow as I do.
Piaget: Of course not. Consciousness in others is impenetrable.
Bringuier: Do you think it is a barrier that will some day be broken down?
Piaget: We may find physiological indications by studying alertness.
Bringuier: How so?
Piaget: Electroencephalographic waves mark moments of attention or alertness in opposition to total passivity. It's possible, then, that the state of consciousness compared to the state of nonconsciousness will be revealed by electrical means.
Bringuier: But that's quantitative and not qualitative?
Piaget: True, but it would be very valuable if it could be applied to animals.
Bringuier: We were just talking about cell behavior. Haven't you ever wanted to study molecular biology?
Piaget: It's a little late. I dropped biology when I was twenty, and I'm too old to go back to it. Of course it would appeal to me.
Bringuier: Why did you drop it?
Piaget: One very practical reason is that I was clumsy. I bungled my work with the microtome.
Bringuier: Do you know why you were clumsy?
Piaget: Oh, as a matter of fact, because it bored me. A person with a systematic interest in a field would develop the necessary skills. Laboratory work in biology requires a lot more patience! Psychology is still such an unknown terrain that one constantly finds new things, and very quickly; whereas in biology—which,

after all, has a hundred years' head start on psychology—it requires more work to find something new. Then, too, I liked ideas, philos . . . *(he corrects himself)* epistemology.

Bringuier: You were going to say philosophy.

Piaget: I was going to say philosophy, but it's a dangerous word.

Bringuier: Why dangerous?

Piaget: Because it is so ambiguous. I was interested in problems of knowledge insofar as they could be approached scientifically, as a biologist would. In order to find a bridge between biology and theory of knowledge, it was necessary to study mental development, the development of intelligence, the genesis of ideas . . .

Bringuier: Yes, that's what you call epistemology: the theory of knowledge, of cognition.

Piaget: I believe that, in order to study epistemology objectively and scientifically, we must not take knowledge with a capital K, as a state in its higher forms, but seek the processes of formation: how one passes from a lesser degree of knowledge to a greater one, relative to the level and to the point of view of the subject. The study of such transformations of knowledge, the progressive adjustment of knowledge, is what I call genetic epistemology. It's the only possible viewpoint for a biologist—or so it seems to me.

Bringuier: What from your early years led you to these studies? What drew your interest? What did your father do?

Piaget: He was a historian.

Bringuier: So you lived in a university community?

Piaget: Yes. He urged me not to study history.

Bringuier: Why?

Piaget: Because it isn't a true science. His objection was that claims cannot be proved.

Bringuier: You get your love of facts from him?

Piaget: Of course.

Bringuier: What were you like as a boy?

Piaget: I began to study zoology very early. I did many studies on mollusks.

Bringuier: When you were still quite young, you found something noteworthy—or, if you prefer, something that had not been noted before—didn't you?

Piaget: I catalogued and studied adaptation.

Bringuier: In a certain little animal that changes form in certain conditions and not in others . . .

Piaget: Yes. The changes in the shell of the lymnaea relative to the agitation of the water.

Bringuier: That was entirely new at the time? No one had studied it?

Piaget: There are mollusk specialists, but not many of them.

Bringuier: And how old were you?

Piaget: I began quite early because, in the little town of Neuchâtel, where I was studying, I happened to have an old teacher who had no assistant. I became his "famulus"—his slave—as he called me. Through him, I learned about mollusks.

Bringuier: Was he a biologist?

Piaget: A zoologist. When he died, I began to work alone and to publish.

Bringuier: You were thirteen or fourteen?[2]

Piaget: Yes.

Bringuier: How did the transition to psychology occur?

Piaget: I wanted to understand the conditions in which knowledge occurs; I was already interested in epistemology. Where general ideas are concerned, mollusks don't take one very far. Moreover, I was reading Kant and Bergson and wanted to find a point where facts and reflection would intersect.

---

2. 1911: "Mollusques du Val d'Herens," *Rameau de sapin,* no. 45; "Les Limnées des lacs de Neuchâtel et Morat," *Journal de conchyliologie.* Piaget's first published article was "Un Moineau albinos," *Rameau de sapin* (1907); he was then eleven.

Bringuier: And what happened?

Piaget: When you begin to study a subject in psychology, you are completely astonished at how little specific information there is. One thing leads to another, and you see what happens.

Bringuier: You worked with Binet in Paris, I think?[3]

Piaget: No, he had died. I worked in his laboratory with his collaborator, Simon, who wasn't living in Paris and couldn't oversee what I did—luckily!

Bringuier: It wasn't orthodox?

Piaget: Not at all. As a result, I worked alone.

Bringuier: Tell me about it.

Piaget: Simon wanted me to standardize in French the tests that had been devised in English. The tests were admirable from the point of view of logical structure. I became interested immediately in the way the child reasoned and the difficulties he encountered, the mistakes he made, his reasons for making them, and the methods he came up with in order to get to the right answers. From the outset, I did what I've been doing ever since: I made qualitative analyses instead of preparing statistics about right and wrong answers.

Bringuier: You were also very young when you wrote a sort of essay called *Recherche,* with a protagonist named Sebastien?

Piaget: Yes.

Bringuier: It was reminiscent of Rousseau, a kind of philosophical essay?

Piaget: Yes. I was clever enough to know that its ideas were debatable, a bit bizarre; if I wanted them to be tolerated, I would have to put them in fictional form.

Bringuier: How old were you?

Piaget: Twenty.

---

3. Alfred Binet's studies in psychology marked the beginning of the use of intelligence tests (Binet-Simon Scale). We shall see later what Piaget himself thinks of tests.

Bringuier: Have you reread it?

Piaget: I don't believe I have. Still, there were some ideas in it that I haven't forgotten: equilibration, assimilation.[4]

Bringuier: Sebastien was you?

Piaget: Yes, he was me.

4. Prodigious unity of mind: he never ceases to refine these first concepts periodically. The idea of equilibration, in particular, was, sixty years later, the subject of a newly published study, *L'Equilibration des structures cognitives,* which became a part of the *Proceedings* of the 1976 symposium (see below).

Insights and Illusions of Philosophy

Piaget goes to his desk every morning, as he has for the past forty years, his mind filled with the idea of the work to be completed.

Piaget: It's never Sunday for me—I work every day.

Bringuier: How long?

Piaget: Four or five pages.

Bringuier: You count in pages, not in hours?

Piaget: Yes, it's been like that for many years, alas!

Bringuier: Do you take vacations?

Piaget: I work on vacations. It's ideal. There aren't any distractions.

Bringuier: Do you go out in the evening or go on trips? For instance, do you ever go to movies?

Piaget: No, never. Well . . . four times. A total of four times!

Bringuier: Four times in your life?

Piaget: Once on an ocean liner—it was ridiculous. Then once in Boulogne, when it was raining—that was just so-so. Twice more, to see Raimu—and that was wonderful. I haven't had time to go again.

Bringuier: What about books or poetry?

Piaget: No poetry at all. I'm completely insensitive to it, or maybe I've never found any that interested me. Novels, yes.

Bringuier: You read novels?

Piaget: I certainly do. Giono's imagination is just fantastic!

Bringuier: And it's not a waste of time, for someone like you? When do you read?

Piaget: Evenings. I don't work in the evening. I read and re-read. I can't tell you how often I've read all the way through Proust.

Bringuier: I don't see what attraction it would hold for you.

Piaget: What? Proust?

Bringuier: Yes.

Piaget: Why, it's as great stuff as epistemology! The way he builds up a character from a series of successive perspectives! Charlus, seen from different points of view . . . I often thought it would be interesting, but I've never had the time, to write the epistemology of Proust; it's very close to Leon Brunschvicg's. They were in school together.

Bringuier: You must do it. It would surprise a lot of people.

Piaget: Maybe.

Bringuier: The first time we talked together, you expressed a certain distrust of philosophical speculation. Isn't the taste for ideas—in your own case in particular—opposed to the modesty and prudence of the scientist you want to be and, indeed, are?

Piaget: I think it's impossible to do anything new in the experimental field unless one is guided by reflection, by ideas.

Bringuier: Then why are you so annoyed with philosophers, who have similar interests?

Piaget: Listen, I have less against philosophers than I would have if I hadn't taught philosophy for four years at the University

of Neuchâtel. But it was while teaching philosophy that I saw
how easily one can say . . . what one wants to say.

Bringuier: You were going to say, "anything at all."

Piaget: I *was* going to say, "anything at all." You can justify a
hypothesis that is basically flawed and offer it as a certainty; you
can . . . In fact, I became particularly aware of the dangers of
speculation, which attracted me. It's a natural tendency. It's so
much easier than digging out facts. You sit in your office and
build a system. It's wonderful! But with my training in biology, I
felt this kind of undertaking was precarious. That doesn't mean I
reject philosophy wholesale. In fact, I wrote a postscript to the
second edition of my little book, *Insights and Illusions of
Philosophy,* because I had learned how to talk to philosophers as
a result of a discussion I had at the Rationalists' Union with
Ricoeur, Jeanson, and others, who gave me some good lessons.
In the postscript I state clearly that I'm deeply indebted to
philosophy. I owe to it my position on problems I've studied, and
I believe that philosophical reflection is indispensable for the
scholar, indispensable for research; but reflection is only a means
of asking questions, not of answering them. Reflection is a
heuristic process, not a means for verification. You see, the two
things must always be distinguished: reflection, as a process of
raising questions; then, the manner of answering them—
particularly, by the use of controls and verification, without
which I think one cannot speak of knowledge. I reproach
philosophy for believing it can attain knowledge, because knowledge, in my opinion, presupposes verification, and verification
always presupposes a delimitation of problems, a delimitation
that enables us to undertake collective verification by means of
controls mutually agreed upon.

Bringuier: I wonder if what you attack in philosophy isn't
what is called metaphysics?

Piaget: Yes, of course.

Bringuier: In your book, *Insights and Illusions of Philosophy,* you talk about certain philosophers and not others. You don't speak of Heidegger, for instance.

Piaget: I discuss those philosophers who have elaborated a theory of knowledge, thus who claim to compete with science on its own ground.

Bringuier: Isn't metaphysics something beyond that? A meditation on Being . . . I don't know whether it is a mode of knowledge, but, if so, it's a quite different mode of knowledge from others—from the knowledge that science permits. Wouldn't you agree? *(Silence.)* Isn't there any knowledge other than scientific knowledge?

Piaget: Let's speak more clearly. What is knowledge? Do you hold that a problem may be susceptible of several contradictory solutions? *(He sees that I accept the formulation.)* Well! What do you mean by knowledge? Give me an example of two metaphysicians who agree without one being a disciple of the other.

Bringuier: I think the religious person, for example, has a knowledge of divinity. He calls it knowledge. Mystics claim to have knowledge of the ineffable.

Piaget: Yes, I see. It's a question of vocabulary and semantics. I have difficulty calling "knowledge" the knowledge held by a group of men, however respected they may be, if their knowledge cannot be shared by others. That's not knowledge; it's belief, by definition. A belief which, moreover, can be rational, respected, and anything else you might suggest. Knowledge begins from the moment it is communicable and controllable.

Bringuier: And measurable?

Piaget: I wouldn't go so far as that. Some knowledge is qualitative. In psychology, in logic, not everything is measurable. But knowledge makes its appearance when there is agreement on controls and on verification by means of successive approximations.

Bringuier: On facts, then?

Piaget: On facts or ideas! I doubt that mathematics can be called fact. If someone makes an error in the demonstration of a theorem, the error will be corrected. You don't find that in metaphysics. Metaphysics hasn't made any progress from Plato to Heidegger—since you mention Heidegger.

Bringuier: Scientists invented the idea of progress.

Piaget: Not only invented the idea of progress but realized some progress!

Bringuier: Because science builds on itself.

Piaget: A scientific theory is quickly outdated, but the theories that follow it benefit from it and consist in improving on it. I don't see this in metaphysics, so it's hard for me to call it knowledge.

(A silence.)

Bringuier: How long has the human mind treated knowledge the way you've just defined it?

Piaget: Why, since the Greeks! I say the Greeks because I'm not sufficiently familiar with the Chinese or the Indians. There may well be other sources.

Bringuier: During the Greek era, philosophy was combined with scientific inquiry?

Piaget: It's well known that the Greek philosophers were serious-minded individuals who studied science.

Bringuier: Descartes, too.

Piaget: Quite right. I have the greatest respect for all the philosophers who studied science.

Bringuier: When did science and philosophy become separated?

Piaget: Essentially in the nineteenth century, I think, because of the tendency of certain scientific minds to try to derive a metaphysic from science. Materialism, for instance. Because their science was not clearly enough distinguished from their metaphysics, the antimaterialists tried to create a mode of knowledge that would go beyond science and would be superior to it and independent of it.

(He is lost in thought.)

From the Greeks to Descartes and Leibniz, philosophy found support in science as far as it could. What was new in the nineteenth century was a sort of parascientific knowledge, elaborated on the fringes of science, independently of it and immediately claiming a higher rank. I find all this disturbing, but it clearly prevails today.

Bringuier: But some philosophers today follow science closely.

Piaget: That's true. Take Desanti, for example; Vuillemin and his group; Granger; and I could name a number of others. But this movement is new by contrast with the existentialism of a generation or two ago. And then, many writers today call philosophy what I myself call scientific epistemology—Desanti, for example, whom I just mentioned. A science is not studied on a single level; you have experimental research, you have the level of theory, of ideas, drawn from the results of research, and you also have the level of epistemological reflection appropriate to this science, bearing on its methods and results. I would set the work of Jean Toussaint Desanti at this third level.

Bringuier: You aren't alone in proclaiming the death of classical philosophy. Doesn't the whole movement of social sciences today support the idea you're proposing, that philosophy can no longer maintain its place and its prerogatives?

Piaget: I think you're right; it's an idea that is, in fact, in the wind. But I distrust popular ideas; you have to sort them out and distinguish serious-minded writers from the ones who write commentaries on each other's work.

*The Child as Model
of Developing Intelligence*

> *Every Saturday, his rucksack on his back, Jean
> Piaget goes for a long bicycle ride in the nearby
> mountains.*

Bringuier: Do you feel that you are very Swiss? Is the fact that
you were born here, that you belong to this country, important
to you?

Piaget: It's very important in the sense that I think a small
country has its advantages, if I may say so. There's a sort of
freedom of thought that seems greater than in large countries.
I'm thinking in terms of scientific work.

Bringuier: How do you mean?

Piaget: It stems from the fact that one doesn't take oneself
seriously. One is less inclined to pontificate. The smaller the
country, the fewer temptations one has.

Bringuier: You travel quite a bit. You often go to America,
don't you?

Piaget: Yes, but I am dismayed by the role there of fashions
and schools of thought. They all do the same thing at a given
moment; then suddenly the fashion changes, and all of them do

something else. Then the same thing happens again. This is true in Russia, as well.

Bringuier: Do you think a researcher should work alone?

Piaget: Oh, no; you must have contacts, and you must, especially, have people who contradict you. You have to have a group. I believe in interdisciplinary research and collective research.

Bringuier: But there has to be flexibility?

Piaget: That's right.

Bringuier: Now we're talking about your craft. First of all, is what you do a craft?

Piaget: Of course.

Bringuier: It's a craft?

Piaget: As soon as you have a technique, you have a craft.

Bringuier: In that case, tell me how you do experimental psychology—and also epistemology, since you refuse to separate the two, if I'm not mistaken.

Piaget: That's right! One can easily dissociate epistemology from psychology if one is interested only in the mental level of the adult, for example. On the one hand, there are questions about the way intelligence functions, and these relate to psychology; on the other hand, there are questions about the value of the instruments of intelligence that are being used—and that's theory of knowledge.

But if you study the *formation* of knowledge, which is my craft, you must constantly identify the intervening factors—those due to external experience, social life, or language and those due to the internal structure of the thinking of the subject, which is constructed as it develops. You see, these are all related epistemological problems that are also related to psychological research.

Bringuier: You've mentioned external factors—that is, environmental factors—and internal factors. Which are the more important?

Piaget: They are perfectly equal in importance. They are indissociable. Knowledge is an interaction between subject and object, and I think the subject cannot be locked in by a structure given once and for all, as the apriorists would have it—as if everything in the mind were predetermined. I think that the subject constructs his knowledge, constructs his structures, and ... we'll be talking more about that.

Bringuier: Is that "freedom"?

Piaget: Yes, of course. My real concern is the explanation of what is new in knowledge from one stage of development to the next. How is it possible to attain something new? That's perhaps my central concern.

Bringuier: How one changes?

Piaget: How one increases one's knowledge by finding something new, relative to the limited knowledge with which one began; but the new thing has to be adapted.

Bringuier: You've worked primarily with children to carry out the work you describe?

Piaget: Yes.

Bringuier: Primarily or exclusively?

Piaget: Exclusively.

Bringuier: Why?

Piaget: If we worked with adults—which would be ideal from the viewpoint of progressive construction—it would mean reconstituting the history of thought. The stages that are most valuable from this perspective, however, are in fact those that are the most unknowable—the prehistoric stages.

Bringuier: Why? Aren't there people all around us?

Piaget: No, no; the people around us have centuries of culture and training behind them.

Bringuier: And so?

Piaget: To study the formation of the human mind as I would have liked to do it, we would have had to reconstruct the stages from monkey to man, the stages of prehistoric man, the stages of fossilized man; but we know only a few techniques for doing that. The beginnings of language, the techniques handed down from one generation to the next—all that unfortunately escapes us.

Bringuier: You seem to be saying that culture—that is, what one finds in man today, modern man—obstructs one's reading of him, as if we had to clean him up.

Piaget: No, it's not that. The problem is to learn how knowledge is formed, how the structures of intelligence are formed. Well, in contemporary man, an enormous number of structures have already been formed, and we don't know their history. No matter what word is used, it has thousands of years of history behind it. It's a concept that has been collectively elaborated over an enormous number of generations. You don't grasp the mode of construction in these cases, you get the product. Products aren't enough for me! Thus, reconstructing history—it can be done as far back as the Greeks, but even then . . . What is wonderful about the child is that you always have an individual starting from scratch, and you can see how all this occurs.

Bringuier: Does the child really start from scratch? He too has an environment, a cultural milieu.

Piaget: Take the baby from birth to approximately eighteen months or two years, when he begins to use speech; it isn't his cultural milieu that lets him discover, for example, the permanence of the object.

Bringuier: What is the "permanence of objects"?

Piaget: The "permanence of the object" refers to the fact that an object that disappears from the field of view is conceived as continuing to exist.

Bringuier: One keeps the idea of it.

Piaget: Not only the idea. The possibility of finding it again. This isn't innate at all. Only when the baby is nine or ten months old, and one hides the object he is about to grasp, does he begin to be able to remove the screen and rediscover the object.

Bringuier: That is, until the tenth month, if he can't see his mother, he believes she doesn't exist.

Piaget: He doesn't believe anything because he has no instruments for thought. But she has disappeared, she has been reabsorbed. The only way to make her return is to shout very loud, but there is no way to localize her in space.

Take the simplest experiment. Give a baby a toy he likes. He reaches out to take it; you lay a handkerchief over it. He takes his hand away—as if the object didn't exist. He doesn't think of lifting the handkerchief. But if you put the handkerchief over his face, he knows very well how to take it off.

Bringuier: At what age does this stop?

Piaget: At eight, nine, ten months. The idea that the object continues to exist, that it can be rediscovered, comes late. It's the basis of our representation of the physical world, but the baby requires months to arrive at this point.

Bringuier: What you describe, what's been observed in contemporary babies, if I may call them that—can one imagine it's been the same for human babies from the beginning?

Piaget: I'm convinced that it applies to human babies from the beginning, and not only to them. My friend Gruber in America ran experiments with kittens and found the same stages, except that the kitten takes only four months to reach the level the baby reaches at nine months. This is interesting, because the kitten doesn't go much farther, whereas the baby continues on to the stage of civilized man.

Bringuier: And why is that?

Piaget: You mean, why has man gone further than the animals? The classic answer is that language and culture, by passing tradition along from one generation to the next, allow the learning period to be shortened. But this isn't a real answer, because we must still ask why.

Bringuier: What is your solution?

Piaget: The shattering of instinct, which was too limited in its programming.

Bringuier: And why did man decide it was too limited?

Piaget: Because of the ecological situation. Take the example of chimpanzees. They begin to climb trees, to walk in a nearly upright position. This creates a series of new problems, you see. Then, if instinct is no longer enough, they just have to find something else.

Bringuier: Where are chimps on the scale?

Piaget: They are superior to one-year-old babies, but they don't progress much beyond that.

Bringuier: They are at the brink . . .

Piaget: At the brink of the symbolic function, yes. There have been some interesting experiments. There are monkeys who have been trained to use tokens for an automatic vending machine. When, out of sight of the machine, a monkey is given some tokens, he carefully lays them aside. If he is given fake tokens, he gets angry; if he has a hungry friend in the next cage, he passes bananas to him or tokens that will allow the friend to get some food. If he mixes a fake token with the others, the friend will throw it at his head. All of this shows that they understand the function of the token apart from the presence of the vending machine.

Bringuier: But the other chimp must also know the function of the vending machine.

Piaget: Of course, but it is already symbolic in this sense.

*Experiments with Children.
The Discovery
of Developmental Stages*

*A bottle half full of colored liquid is placed on
a table. A child is asked to draw what he sees.
He does so.*

*Then the bottle is tilted, so that it stands at
an angle to the table. The child is asked to
make another drawing, again "by copying
what he sees." The child draws the table and
the tilted bottle; the line indicating the level of
the liquid inside is drawn at right angles to the
bottle, as in the original position.*

*Every time the experiment is run, the same
"error" is made.*

Bringuier: Let's go back to your actual work, to your methods.
How do you work? What happens?

Piaget: Ah! I have some fine collaborators. At the beginning of
the year I suggest a program of experiments, and it is often
further developed by the team members, who add new ideas to
it. The students help too, which gives them some training. The
experiments are coordinated and complement one another.

Bringuier: The raw material that comes to you is a set of con-versations?

Piaget: A series of informal conversations with the children, on topics we've chosen; from them we derive protocols that are the written results of the conversations.

Bringuier: How long does a study last?

Piaget: Usually a year.

Bringuier: How can you tell when it's finished?

Piaget: I have only one criterion. I consider an investigation finished when we no longer find out anything new, that's all. When the new protocols we collect repeat what we already know, we take up a new subject.

Bringuier: So from this raw material you write books?

Piaget: Yes, alas.

Bringuier: Why alas?

Piaget: I mean alas for the reader.

Bringuier: Let's go back to the content of these conversations. Are they a kind of test?

Piaget: No. A test is related to performance, to results. We're interested in how the child reasons and how he discovers new tools, so we use direct conversation, informal conversation.

Bringuier: Is a test always a kind of examination?

Piaget: An examination, yes, and especially a standardization. You ask, you select, you fix the questions in advance. How can we, with our adult minds, know what will be interesting? If you follow the child wherever his answers lead spontaneously, in-stead of guiding him with preplanned questions, you can find out something new . . . Of course, there are three or four questions we always ask, but beyond that we can explore the whole area in-stead of sticking to fixed questions.

Bringuier: But surely, some questions have to be included in order to produce statistics. *(Piaget wrinkles his nose.)* Just to have a coherent body of information.

Piaget: Exactly. Once the work of clearing away, of groundbreaking, has been done, which consists of discovering new things and finding things that hadn't been anticipated, you can begin to standardize—at least if you like that sort of thing—and to produce accurate statistics. But I find it more interesting to do the work of groundbreaking.

Bringuier: And you're not afraid the individual cases will be too individual?

Piaget: Why, no. What's so remarkable is that the answers show an unbelievable convergence. While you were preparing this interview, I was classifying the new documents that just came. Twenty-five kids I don't know, and they all say the same thing! At the same age!

Bringuier: Because they're from the same social class and the same city?

Piaget: I don't think so.

Bringuier: Because they're at the same level of evolution?

Piaget: Yes.

Bringuier: I think this brings us to one of your main ideas: that children, regardless of their society and their historical period, go through a series of stages in the evolution of intelligence that is always the same.

Piaget: It's the same because each stage is necessary to the following one. It's called a "sequential order."

Bringuier: Each stage allows the next stage to occur?

Piaget: That's right. It becomes probable, whereas at the beginning it wasn't. Now that can be verified easily enough anywhere, though there will be cases of delay or acceleration.

Bringuier: The order stays the same?

Piaget: Yes.

Bringuier: Now, what is the order? What are the major stages?

Piaget: Well, there are different levels. Sensory-motor intelligence, before language. Then you have . . .

Bringuier: That's in the infant?

Piaget: Yes, the infant. Then the semiotic function appears—language, symbolic play, mental images, and so forth, up until about the age of seven—which permits the representation of thought, but it is a preoperational thought. There are as yet no operations in the sense I'll define later. The operations I call "concrete" begin at around age seven; they apply directly to objects and are defined as being internalized or internalizable and reversible; that is, they can go in either direction. Addition and subtraction are examples of this. Then come formal operations, which no longer relate directly to objects . . .

> *Everything began for Jean Piaget when he was watching a ten-month-old baby at play:*

I watched him playing with a ball. It was before my own children were born. The ball rolled under an armchair; he went looking for it and found it. He threw it again. It disappeared under a deep sofa with a fringe. He couldn't find the ball. Then he went back to the armchair, where he had found it before.

For him the object isn't completely localizable. It's still part of the action that was successful. It isn't yet a body moving independently, which, being under the couch, couldn't be under the armchair. Later it becomes a body moving independently, and the child looks for it in terms of its localizations. Then you can speak of the permanence of the object—what we mentioned the other day.

> *A ball that wasn't where it "should" have been. From this banal occurrence, this incident of daily life, Jean Piaget went on to derive his fundamental intuitions regarding the psychology of intelligence. An adult finds "absurd" the behavior of the baby–the baby who, however, prefigures in a certain way the man he will become. Where is the threshold . . . where are the thresholds?*
>
> *At this point the scholar and his collaborators are engaged in various experiments. They are in a room at the International Center for Genetic*

*Epistemology. A young woman[1] and a little
blonde girl sit facing each other.*

Nadine, aged five

—When's your birthday?

—I don't know.

—Have you been five a long time?

—Yes.

—Look, we're going to play games. Tell me what this is. What is it? I know you've used them before—they're little checkers. What color are they?

—Some are green and some are red.

—Green and red. Which are prettier?

—The red ones.

—The red ones. So I'll be green. Watch what I'm going to do. I'm putting my green checkers like this. There. You see? I'm lining them up. Now you take the little red checkers and put them below mine. Like I did.[2] There, very good. Now, tell me, what do you think? Are there just as many red pieces as green ones? Are they the same? Or maybe there are more green ones? What do you think? More red ones? *(Nadine hesitates.)* If you look at the greens and then at the reds, are there more greens or more reds?

—They're both the same.

—All right. They're the same. How did you know?

—There aren't more greens or reds.

—There aren't more greens or reds! Fine. Now watch what I'm going to do. *(She spreads out the red checkers.)* Now, tell me if there's the same number of greens and reds. No? Which has more?

—The reds.

—There are more reds. Why?

—Because you changed them.

1. The questioner is Catherine Dami, assistant at the Center.

2. It is part of the "conversation" technique to follow, and imitate if necessary, the child's way of speaking so that he will feel the distance from the adult as little as possible.

—I changed them, yes. But how do you know there are more reds?

—Because the greens are closer together.

—But Nadine, suppose we counted them. If we counted them with a finger, how many would there be? Would there be the same number of reds and greens, or would they be different?

—They'd be the same!

—Let's put them back the way they were before. *(She does so.)* How are they now?

—They're the same.

—And if you count them, what do you get?

—There's the same number.

—That's good. Now we're going to change the greens. What have we got now?

—The reds are closer together than the greens.

—Yes. And if we counted them, would there be more reds? Or more greens? Or would they be the same?

—No.

—What would we get?

—Because the greens are spread out more and the reds are closer together.

—Yes. So, what do we have? More greens, or more reds, or the same of each?

—More greens.

—More greens this time. What do we have to do to make them the same again?

—Have to put them like they were before.

—Have to put them like they were before. Like that, they're alike now? Okay, now we'll play with something else.

Taïma, aged six

—Do you know when your birthday is?

—I already had it. May first.

—Mine's in June, I told you a few minutes ago. Do you see these two balls? Do you know what they're made of?

—Modeling clay.

—Modeling clay, yes. And what color are they?

—Red.

—And the other one?

—White.

—It's white. Now look at the two balls of modeling clay and tell me if they're both the same size. Do they both have the same amount of clay in them?

—Yes.

—They're the same?

—Yes.

—Are you sure, or are you not very sure?

—No.

—You're not very sure? Do you think one of them is bigger than the other? Is there more clay in one of them?

(Taïma hesitates, then makes up her mind.)

—No.

—So they're both the same? Now do you know what we're going to do? We're going to say it's cake—not really, but just pretend. You take the red cake, and I'll take the white. If we eat them, we'll both eat the same amount?

—Yes.

—Yes. Okay, now watch. I'm going to take my cake and do something with it. Tell me what I'm doing. Look. What is it?

—It's a stick.

—A stick. Now, what do you think? If I eat this stick, and you eat your clay ball, will we both eat the same amount, or does one of us have more to eat than the other?

—You have more to eat than I do.

—Yes? Why?

—Because that's longer than this.

—Okay. And suppose I make it longer—you see, even longer—you see, like this?

—You'll have more.

—I still have more to eat than you do?

—Yes.

—If I take it again and make it into a ball, like I had a minute ago—like it was at the beginning—how much will we each have to eat?

—The same.

—The same?

—Yes.

—All right. Now we'll take your ball. Look, I'm going to flatten it out like this. What shall we call this, what I just made?

—A steak.

—A steak? Well, okay. It's a funny color for a steak. Not cooked yet, right?

—Yes.

—Now, you eat your steak and I'll eat my ball. Do we both have the same amount to eat? Or does one of us have more?

—Yes. *(Taïma smiles and points to herself.)*

—You have more? Why?

—Because mine's fatter than yours.

—Fatter. But yours is so thin. Look.

—It's bigger.

—Bigger. So you really have more, do you?

—Yes.

—Is that right? Is it right? Are you sure?

—Yes.

—But when yours was a ball too—when it was a ball like this one—how much did we have, each of us?

—The same.

—The same? So now it's changed?

—Yes.

—And to make them the same again, what do we have to do?

—Have to make it into a ball again.

—Your clay?

—Yes.

Sophie, aged six

—Tell me, Sophie, would you like to play with the scales?
—Yes.
—Okay. Now look: do these two balls weigh the same?
—No.
—I don't think so either. Which is heavier?
—This one.
—This one. I want them to be exactly the same. Look now.
—This is lower than that.
—I'm going to take off another little piece. Is that it, now?
—Yes.
—Yes. How can you tell they weigh the same?
—Because I saw it there.
—You watched the pointer?
—Yes.
—That means they weigh the same? We'll take them off the scales. We'll make a long stick with the red one, and we'll leave your ball like it is. If I weigh them now—if I put them back on the scales—what would we see?
—This one would be heavier.
—Why?
—Because—because it's lighter when you make it like that.
—Are you sure? Like this?
—Yes.
—Why is it lighter when you roll it out like this? Because we didn't try it, did we?
—Because this one's thin and this one's fat.
—Now I see. And suppose I rolled this one back into a ball, how would it be?
—It would be heavier.
—Suppose I made two balls and weighed them, how would they be?
—The same.
—The same? Are you sure?

—Yes.

—How do you know?

—Because they are the same balls.

> *Resumption of our conversation at the home of Jean Piaget. We begin to talk about these experiments.*

Piaget: Yes, for the little ones there is more clay than before because it is longer.

Bringuier: Or shorter!

Piaget: Or less because it's thinner. Never both at once. When they see one dimension, they don't see the other. Whereas, at a certain level, they see both and see the compensation: it's longer, therefore thinner, so it's the same. But this presupposes reversibility.

Bringuier: Then they understand that matter is conserved.

Piaget: First, matter; then, a year or two later, with the same arguments, weight; and finally, volume. Volume measured by the level of water displaced if you drop a pellet or clay sausage into a glass of water.

Bringuier: But it's funny they start with matter.

Piaget: Yes, it's quite something, because matter without weight or volume can't be perceived.

Bringuier: A pure concept.

Piaget: Required by the principle of conservation. Yes, a pure concept. As Poincaré used to say, "Something has to be conserved, or reasoning is not possible," but we don't know ahead of time what it is.

Bringuier: Before we go on, I want to say something about the experiments. Your collaborators have told me that a reversal occurs if the stick of modeling clay is made even longer.

Piaget: That's right. The child says, "There's more because it's longer"; but suddenly that doesn't work any more, and he says, "It's too thin, there's less than before!"

Bringuier: But he can see perfectly well that it's the same operation, continued.

Piaget: Of course!

Bringuier: It isn't logical.

Piaget: No, not at all. That's all prelogical.[3] And then, too, there's something in the conversations that I find very interesting. The argument often goes like this: It's the same amount; it hasn't changed, because you haven't taken anything away. The little ones knew very well you hadn't taken any of it away! But that was no argument for them. Whereas it becomes an argument. There you have a transformation of structure. It becomes necessary. It's the Kantian a priori—but at the end, not at the beginning. Necessity at the end and not at the beginning.[4]

(A silence.)

Bringuier: That's enough about the experiments. As regards these structures, do you think the child—whom you've been studying for a good many years now—is universal, over time and also geographically? Because, in fact, you've worked primarily with Swiss children, and mostly with children from Geneva.

Piaget: That's a big problem, which presupposes some very difficult research, because comparative child psychology requires you to go to remote societies and master their languages—that's the domain of ethnographers and anthropologists; but at the same time, you have to know the interview technique. The technique takes months to learn. The interviewer must have an ethnographer's training in order to go into a different society, and he must have a psychologist's technique in order to know how to interview. So far, we've seen, on the one hand, anthropologists who thought they were reproducing experiments,

3. This remark of Piaget's, coming, after all, at the end of the discussion, left me with the impression that a door had been opened. The very tranquillity of his comment, its matter-of-fact tone, were probably what brought me face to face with what it meant—brought it home to me. Clearly, the child's reasoning did not rest on an inarticulate or poorly formulated logic; it wasn't a clumsy attempt at adult logic. It owed nothing to that logic. It rested instead on something else, another world—a world that Piaget had been exploring for a long time. From what he said, I sensed the dimensions, the true perspective, of his research—or at least believed that I did.

4. See below, p. 77.

for instance, but it was done very superficially, and, on the other hand, well-trained people in psychology who didn't know the children's language and had to conduct the interviews through interpreters. So, broadly speaking, what we've found up until now is remarkable agreement, but with accelerations and delays, as I've mentioned before. To give an example of a delay, I had a student who worked in Teheran. The children of Teheran are at about the same level, at the same ages, as children in Geneva, but the ones in the rural areas, who are illiterate, show two, three, or four years' delay in passing through the same stages; that's the main thing.

Bringuier: In the same order?

Piaget: Yes, of course. The stages are an order of succession. It isn't the average age. But much comparative work has been done. Miss Churchill did some experiments. I just saw a psychologist from Canberra who did conversation experiments with the Aruntas of Australia—you know, the tribe in the middle of Australia. Well, she found the same things, but with a *décalage* [phase difference]. Then there are the Canadians—Laurendeau, Pinard, and Boisclair—who did experiments in Martinique. Children in Martinique are in the French school system until they earn their elementary-school certificate. They do get through, but in my studies of operations and conversations they are four years behind.

Bringuier: What causes that?

Piaget: Their society, which is lazy. The father of one of these children had just built a house. When it was finished, he realized he had forgotten to put in the stairs.

Bringuier: And your impression is that the surroundings become more important as the child gets older?

Piaget: Certainly![5]

5. Since then, a number of comparative research studies have been done in Africa by five or six psychologists from Geneva, under the direction of B. Inhelder.

Bringuier: But, if that is so, how true is the current theory—which comes from psychoanalysis—that says that everything is completed in the first three years?

Piaget: No! Cognitively, it isn't so. No, no! They're exaggerating. Oh, no! New constructions occur during adolescence.

Structures. Their Mechanisms. Assimilation and Accommodation

The problem of the genesis of structures is the principal problem in science today.
Ilia Prigogine, physicist. Lecture at the International Center for Genetic Epistemology

The structure regulates itself within its own boundaries in such a way as to be able to extend them indefinitely. Is this clear?
Jean Piaget. Statement at a seminar at the Center

In constantly mobile equilibrium, always hovering at the edge of its own metamorphosis, it is in every living system that which resists and submits, transmitting to the whole those progressive readjustments that alone allow survival.
Letter from a Japanese student after a stay at the Center

When one knows how to do one addition, one knows how to do them all.
Rafel Carreras, physicist, speaking in a hallway at the Center

Bringuier: You've used the word "structures" several times in reference to the development of intelligence. Do you think of yourself as a structuralist?

Piaget: You might say so, although it seems to me there's a basic difference from popular structuralisms, which assume pre-formed or predetermined structures, given once and for all—and consciousness of them comes later. I think that all structures are constructed; the basic fact about them is the process of their construction, and at the beginning nothing more is "given" than some few points that support the rest. But structures are not given in advance, neither in the human mind nor in the external world as we perceive and organize it. They are constructed by the interaction between the individual's activities and the object's reactions.

Bringuier: Your reasoning is the same as for the stages. It's a sequential order.

Piaget: Yes, of course. For every stage, every level, there is a corresponding set of structures, so, naturally, the movement is the same. From the moment life appears . . .

Bringuier: Are there stages and structures in the organism, just as in the mind?

Piaget: Why, yes. In organic development, you have stages—without a shadow of doubt—which are classic and well known in embryogenesis.

Bringuier: Even in the developing fetus.

Piaget: That's right. Any species. The embryological stages are sequential, in the sense that each is necessary to the appearance of the following one. And presupposes the preceding one. In other words, no stage can be skipped. Well, now, I believe that the same thing appears in the stages of development of the cognitive functions of intelligence.

Bringuier: Of thought?

Piaget: Of thought.

Bringuier: But, unless I'm mistaken, there is still a big difference: on the organic side, the stages of development are predetermined from the outset by the genetic system; but this is not so in the structures of thought, not in the evolution of thought.

Piaget: Yes. I believe the difference is one of degree, because in embryogenesis, of course, there is an inherited program, but the effect of the environment increases. Waddington showed clearly that its system is different from the genetic system. He calls it the "epigenetic system," from the noun "epigenesis," which is the idea that the embryo constructs something and that not everything is preformed; then, the epigenetic system presupposes interactions with the environment. It isn't complete predetermination.

Bringuier: Fetuses all develop in the same way!

Piaget: Not exactly; individual differences can be observed. Even if fetal development is regular as a whole, there are necessary interactions with the environment, interactions that presuppose aliments, so to speak; because, if they aren't there, malformations will occur. It's a difference of degree, not at all a difference of kind.

Bringuier: And this is also true of animals?

Piaget: Certainly.

Bringuier: Still, doesn't everything appear to be given from the start by the genetic code, by the genetic system?

Piaget: That is not true even in the domain of instinct, because there is always a measure of individual accommodation.

Bringuier: I mean, a bird knows how to make a nest without ever having learned to do it.

Piaget: Yes, of course. There is a genetic program, but circumstances vary considerably; applying the program to circumstances already means a degree of individual accommodation going beyond pure heredity.

Bringuier: It isn't the group itself that adapts?

Piaget: The new generation of ethologists no longer speak of innate behavior. They say "behavior formerly called innate," because there is always, of course, the hereditary program; but there is also an element of practice, of real adaptation, which increases greatly with the acquired behavior of intelligence. *(Si-*

lence.) And when we speak of group behavior, it's . . . instinct is essentially transindividual. That is, male instinct correlates with female instinct; among social animals the various functions are correlated; and so forth. For us, behavior is individual, and, of course, at the same time, it's coordinated with other individuals.[1]

Bringuier: But in the last analysis, what in man is coded?

Piaget: It's very difficult to say, because from the time the maturation of the nervous system was first discussed, no one has ever been able to put his finger on something really hereditary. We are sure that heredity plays a role throughout, that maturation as a factor is entirely present all the time; but nothing positive can be said about what it contributes. It offers possibilities. We know that a certain behavior, impossible at one degree of maturation, becomes possible later, but we cannot say, "This is hereditary, this is not."

Bringuier: Then, from the point of view you're describing, there is a move away from the earlier biological determinism?

Piaget: I wouldn't say "determinism," I would say "predetermination." Today it's constructivism that appears to be preferred across the board. Take the domain of knowledge; when you

1. On reviewing all the conversations for this book, one is struck by the obstinacy with which Piaget battles—and has probably always battled—against what he considers to be an overestimate of the role of the innate. On second thought, it is natural: the need for symmetry between the cognitive structures and the biological structures leads him to reduce to a minimum the extent and the power of what can be considered to be the proper role of biological organization—that is, the genetic program—and, reciprocally, within the biological organization itself, to extend as far as possible the creative role of behavior, which is for him the principal motor for evolution. Likewise, one can shed some light on a significant change in point of view between the two periods of conversations. In 1969 he considered the fruitful period of ontogenesis to be adolescence (see p. 35). In 1975 he seemed to prefer early childhood; but this is because early childhood exhibits structures *in action,* prior to language. It is easier to see them as uninterrupted development beyond organic structures; and, because language appears only after them, if they are found rich enough, one need not make, or need no longer make, language into a privileged boundary, beyond which the higher levels of consciousness would be elaborated. In terms of a discussion current today, any reduction of the boundary between nature and culture contributes to the system's consistency.

consider the history of mathematics, it is, without a shadow of doubt, a continual creation; and when you see the development of the child, there is no doubt that from twelve to fifteen years of age the structures are really astonishingly new and richer compared to the sensory-motor structures, the original structures.

Bringuier: Besides, it's a paradox about structure . . .

Piaget: Of course.

Bringuier: that it is presented as a closed whole.

Piaget: Yes, but at the same time, it is the point of departure for new structures. The real problem is the creation of the new structures.

That's where genesis intervenes. Genesis is the formation of a structure, but it's a potential of the structure itself. If one fails to see that the structure is always a system of transformations—passing from the simpler to the more complex—one cannot understand the passage from one structure to the next, because of the paradox you mentioned. The word "transformation" implies a possible construction of new structures, the enlarging of the initial structure that inserts itself in a more general structure as a particular case. Once number is constructed, for example, there is, first, the discovery of negative numbers, then fractions. The initial structure is incorporated into later ones thanks to genesis, because it is a system of transformations. Genesis presupposes structure because it is never an absolute beginning but always departs from a simpler structure. The two terms are, consequently, absolutely interdependent and indissociable. Genesis is the formation of functions; structure is their organization.

Bringuier: How do you know, experimentally, that you are dealing with a structure? In what form is it encountered?

Piaget: How do we define it? It's the new feeling arising in the individual's consciousness, a feeling of *necessity*. It's the links that, considered simply as given or observed, are experienced as necessary. The individual can't think otherwise. Take transitivity as an example. If $A = B$, if the child then observes that $B = C$, does $A = C$? One can, for instance, ask a child to compare a stick of a certain weight with a rod of the same weight, then with a ball. For the child at the preoperatory level, before the construction of structures, there is no relationship among the three objects. He says he doesn't know. He saw A and B; he saw B and C, but he didn't see A and C together. Or he draws a conclusion about what he believes to be possible or probable. A child at the level of structures finds it obvious, necessary. He smiles and shrugs his shoulders at being asked such a simple question: if $A = B$ and $B = C$, then, obviously, $A = C$. Necessity is the criterion of the structure's closure, the achievement of a structure.

Bringuier: Does this mean that there's a structure only when the child begins to do operations, for example?

Piaget: Before operations—if you accept our definition of them as internalized actions—there are already structures of action. At the sensory-motor level, before language, you already have structures, some even very highly developed. At the sensory-motor level, a structure is, for instance, a group of displacements: the infant can displace an object from one spot to another.

Bringuier: At what age?

Piaget: From six months. The infant can put an object back where it came from. He can take detours to arrive at his goal; that's at the beginning of his second year. When he learns to walk, he can toddle around, following the layout of rooms or the garden. Simultaneously, he is making compositions of displacements, he's backtracking to the point of departure and making detours. Detours represent associativity of the displacement group. It's a geometrical structure well known to geometricians. Then, his learning period complete, the individual goes further and internalizes his sensory-motor actions in new structures that are genuine structures of thought. At this point he begins to make classifications: series, whole number, displacement groups by measuring space, and geometrical structures generally; this occurs at about age seven.

The psychological sign of structure is the existence of invariants—what mathematicians call "group invariants."

Invariance is conservation. The ball of clay, the numbers that remain the same even when the elements are separated, when the row is lengthened . . .

Bringuier: But while the structure takes place, if I may put it that way, does genesis stop? Is it immobilized?

Piaget: Not at all. The functioning of the structure is a stage of equilibrium in genesis, the functioning that will lead further, to the construction of other structures. The need for structures is linked to a need for internal consistency and organization, without which there would be internal anarchy, disorder, and inconsistency. As for genesis, it's a problem that is raised whenever the subject faces a new situation. He has to construct something, cope with the problems. Intelligence is, by definition, adaptation to new situations, so there is a continual construction of structures.

Bringuier: We might say, one must assimilate and accommodate—to borrow your expressions.

Piaget: Yes, that's functional language.

Bringuier: Would you explain what assimilation is and what accommodation is?

Piaget: Well, assimilation is just the proof that structures exist. It's the fact that a stimulus from the external world, any excitant, can act on or modify behavior only to the degree that it is integrated with prior structures. Assimilation is chiefly a biological concept. By digesting food, the organism assimilates the environment; this means that the environment is subordinated to the internal structure and not the reverse.

Bringuier: If I eat a cabbage, I don't become a cabbage—is that it?

Piaget: Yes. A rabbit that eats a cabbage doesn't become a cabbage; it's the cabbage that becomes rabbit—that's assimilation. It's the same thing at the psychological level. Whatever the stimulus is, it is integrated with internal structures.

Bringuier: How about accommodation?

Piaget: There is no assimilation without accommodation be-

cause the scheme of assimilation is general, and as soon as it's
applied to a particular situation, it must be modified according to
the particular circumstances of the situation. This is true at every
level. Take, for example, an infant who's just discovered he can
grasp what he sees; well, from then on, everything he sees is
assimilated to the schemes of prehension, that is, it becomes an
object to grasp as well as an object to look at or an object to
suck on. But if it's a large object, for which he needs both hands,
or if it's a very small object and he has to tighten the fingers of
only one hand to grasp it, he will modify the scheme of prehension.

Bringuier: And he changes his effort?

Piaget: He changes his adjustment. That is what I call
"accommodation"—the adjustment of the scheme to the particular situation.

Bringuier: He changes his gesture to suit . . .

Piaget: the object—that's right. Accommodation is determined
by the object, whereas assimilation is determined by the subject.
Then, just as there is no accommodation without assimilation—
because it is always accommodation to something being assimilated to one scheme or another—similarly, there can be no assimilation without accommodation, because the assimilatory
scheme is general and must always be accommodated to the particular situation. I used the example of the infant, but it's also
true for the scholar and the scientist. You have a theory; that's
an assimilatory scheme. You can adapt it to very diverse situations. In mechanics, the same principles of conservation of
movement are used for situations that are quite different. The
adjustment of the assimilatory scheme to all these situations is
accommodation.

Bringuier: It's adaptation?

Piaget: Yes. But I prefer the term "adaptation" for the equilibrium between assimilation and accommodation. Because in
adaptation there are always two poles: you have the pole of
subject-assimilation and the pole of object-accommodation. I

prefer these terms because they show better the dissociation of the subject and the object. There are always two poles. If you simply say "adaptation," without clarification, it gives the impression that it's directed toward the object, determined toward the object. Actually, adaptation is a whole whose two poles can't be dissociated. Assimilation and accommodation.

Bringuier: What about equilibration? You've linked that term with the other two.

Piaget: It refers to assimilation and accommodation in a specific relation with each other; it may be stable. In an intelligent act there is an equilibrium because the two do not hurt each other but rather support each other.

Bringuier: Why "equilibration" and not simply "equilibrium"?

Piaget: Because it's a process, not a balance of forces. Equilibrium is a return to the former state.

Bringuier: Equilibration is dynamic?

Piaget: Yes. It's the self-regulation I spoke of a moment ago. An equilibrated system is a system in which all the errors have been corrected, the excesses compensated for. It isn't a static equilibrium like an immobile balance scale; it's the regulating of behavior.

Bringuier: An equilibrium continually trying to improve itself.

Piaget: Physicists call it a "displacement of equilibrium." Because it isn't ever perfect, and new external factors are always entering the picture and disturbing it.

Bringuier: It's always a question of reacting, and that's what . . .

Piaget: Exactly. The process leads toward equilibrium. But, since equilibrium is never attained—thank heavens!—because the whole world would have had to be assimilated . . .

Bringuier: We're always chasing it.

Piaget: We're always chasing it, and that is science. Once it is caught . . . well, we'll talk about this again later, but I don't believe mankind will ever do it.

Bringuier: Ever?

Piaget: What is completion? Mathematics completed would be . . . *(A silence.)*

Bringuier: But, listening to you I get the impression that the child suddenly changes intellectually, as if there are sudden mutations.

Piaget: No, the transformation is slow. What is sudden is the final comprehension when the structure is completed. You often see this kind of sudden comprehension during an interrogation. A child muddles about and suddenly he sees the light: "Ah, now I understand," and he says something completely unrelated to his remarks at the beginning of the interrogation.

Bringuier: That's wonderful!

Piaget: Yes, and of course it presupposes a whole preliminary labor, underneath, of which the child had no consciousness; but taking consciousness [*prise de conscience*] is sudden. Suddenly he sees things in the external world in a wholly new way. That's what's sudden—not the construction, but the taking of consciousness.

Bringuier: This is the kind of thing you discover in the reports that come in from the members of your team?

Piaget: That's true now. For a long time I did the questioning myself, of course.

Bringuier: Why don't you do it any more?

Piaget: I don't have the time. To make progress with an inquiry, you have to follow it closely. My method is to draw up provisional and hypothetical wording as it proceeds. That provokes further ideas. But I have to do it myself, and that takes more and more of my time.

Bringuier: Ideas . . . experiments based on ideas, which themselves provide you with further ideas?

Piaget: Yes, that's right.

Bringuier: Did you enjoy doing the questioning yourself?

Piaget: Very much. It was exciting. And sometimes I miss doing it. I did it for years in the schools in Geneva, every afternoon. And in Paris, when I was a student in Binet's laboratory. That was in an elementary school. Every afternoon I went to see the children from seven to twelve years old.

Bringuier: Do you like children?

Piaget: Very much.

Bringuier: Because they are guinea pigs?

Piaget: Oh, no! They're alive, it's wonderful. They're new. Oh, no; they're remarkable!

Bringuier: But they can hardly surprise you any more—you know everything they're going to say.

Piaget: No, it just doesn't work out that way. As soon as you start a new series of experiments, there are surprises. Our method is mainly to continue interviewing until we can see the process itself.

Bringuier: And to follow the child?

Piaget: To follow him. To follow him in each answer. This is the way one sometimes finds real surprises.

Bringuier: Is the order of the questions important?

Piaget: Very. Very, because if you're so imprudent as to ask certain questions that suggest and condition the rest, you can no longer see clearly. The questions must be asked in such a way as to avoid verbal "leading."

Bringuier: So the child won't guess the right answers.

Piaget: Yes. And it isn't easy. It takes months of training.

Bringuier: Does it take special talent?

Piaget: It takes great tact. You have to be able to excite the child, to interest him, and yet not suggest anything to him. Beginners often fail to interest the child—they make him yawn—or else they press him with suggestions. They tell him what answers to give.

Bringuier: There's something I wondered about as I thought back over our conversations: does regression occur? I mean, when a new structure appears, when a higher stage appears in the child's consciousness, is there, maybe not annihilation, but at least partial destruction of preceding structures?

Piaget: I wouldn't say destruction, but disequilibrium, which can lead to temporary regression. No doubt about it. If a fact that is too new cannot be integrated immediately, by adjusting the structures, there can be temporary regression. But this isn't true of the child alone. Take the famous story of Driesch, in biology, who discovered regulation in the development of the embryo at the level of the blastula. He discovered that by cutting the egg in half he got two embryos; he was so astounded that he didn't believe it could be explained by the schemes of causal embryology, and he went back to Aristotle's ideas! He began to talk about entelechy and finally quit biology to become a philosophy professor. In my humble opinion, that's a slight regression. *(He smiles, and explains.)* In any case, the appeal to entelechy is a regression. Driesch's discovery was the point of departure for all causal embryology, but Driesch's theory was abandoned immediately. Then they looked for . . .

Bringuier: In a way, temporary regression is the price you pay . . . for new attainments.

Piaget: That's right. When reequilibration does not occur rapidly, there may be a regression with, later, a new departure.

Bringuier: I thought there was always regression to the degree that there was reorganization.

Piaget: No. Reorganization does not imply regression. Reorganization . . .

Bringuier: But it is necessarily the abandonment of certain things.

Piaget: No, not necessarily. In physics, sometimes, when a poor theory is rejected in favor a better one—in that case there is abandonment of something. But never in mathematics. Euclidean geometry did not become even slightly "false" when non-Euclidean geometries were discovered; it was simply integrated into a larger structure as a particular case. The error lay in believing that it was general; it became a particular case—a particular case among other structures—and there wasn't a shadow of regression. Nor of abandonment. Not a single one of Euclid's theorems was abandoned.

Bringuier: It's the very image of progress.

Piaget: Progress in mathematics is always an enrichment, whereas progress in the experimental sciences often entails the abandoning of false hypotheses.

Bringuier: Then, there is another aspect of structures that I don't understand. You seem to say that a child's evolution, a child's intelligence, recalls or evokes or copies or imitates—I don't know what word to use—the progress of mankind generally. Am I wrong? You seem to be saying that the child repeats the history of intellectual man.

Piaget: We musn't exaggerate the parallel between history and individual development,[2] but in broad outline there certainly are stages that are the same. In history, you must begin with material techniques before coming to reflection and representation and scientific explanation. In the domain of causality, which we're now studying, take the first explanations of the pre-Socratics, the first Greek physicists; it's very like what we find the child doing when he begins to understand that matter is conserved—that, when sugar melts, little bits of it continue to exist in the water and, if all the little bits were brought together again, they would make sugar again.

2. Six years later I found him, on the contrary, even more committed to the idea of this parallel, so much so that he was writing a book on it. It is the subject of the ninth conversation (1975).

Knowledge and Affectivity

Bringuier: Now, your approach to the problem of human evolution and stages is strictly from the point of view of intelligence, isn't it?

Piaget: Yes.

Bringuier: You don't deal with the affective level at all?

Piaget: Only because I'm not interested in it. I'm not a psychologist. I'm an epistemologist. *(He smiles, as if he had played a trick on me.)*

Bringuier: Still, you practice experimental psychology?

Piaget: Because I want facts.

Bringuier: And you don't find facts at the level of affect?

Piaget: The problem doesn't interest me as a scientific inquiry because it isn't a problem of knowledge, which is my specialty; and then, too, all the theories produced about affectivity seem to me totally provisional, awaiting the time physiologists will give us accurate endocrinological explanations.

Bringuier: That is, facts.

Piaget: That's right—facts.

Bringuier: But how can one be interested in someone—in a child, to be specific—with regard to his intelligence, the development of his intelligence alone, and not be interested in his affective side? Can they be separated?

Piaget: Obviously, for intelligence to function, it must be motivated by an affective power. A person won't ever solve a problem if the problem doesn't interest him. The impetus for everything lies in interest, affective motivation.

Bringuier: You like one thing, you dislike something else.

Piaget: That provides the motivation, of course. But take, for instance, two boys and their arithmetic lessons. One boy likes them and forges ahead; the other thinks he doesn't understand math; he feels inferior and has all the typical complexes of people who are weak in math. The first boy will learn more quickly, the second more slowly. But, for both, two and two are four. Affectivity doesn't modify the acquired structure at all. If the problem at hand is the construction of structures, affectivity is essential as a motivation, of course, but it doesn't explain the structures.

Bringuier: It's strange that affectivity doesn't appear at the level of structures, regardless! An individual is a whole.

Piaget: Yes, but in the study of feelings, when you find structures, they are structures of knowledge. For example, in feelings of mutual affection there's an element of comprehension and an element of perception. That's all cognitive. In behavior you have—and I think all scholars are agreed on this point—a structure of behavior and a motivating force of behavior. There is motivation on the one hand, and mechanism on the other.

Bringuier: And you're interested in the mechanism.

Piaget: That's right, yes.

Bringuier: But if everyone conforms to structures, as you say, you lose sight of individuality, of the unique qualities of each person.

Piaget: You're forgetting what I told you about accommodation. There is great diversity in structures. And the same structures, implied by different individuals...

Bringuier: Everyone has his own style of accommodation...

Piaget: Of course. Accommodation gives rise to unlimited differentiations. The same structures are very general. The fact that number is the same for everyone, and the series of whole numbers is the same for everyone, doesn't prevent mathematicians, taken one by one, from being unique as individuals. There is such diversification of structures . . .

> ("Of course," I thought to myself, "of course . . . But can a person be reduced to 'accommodation'? Even if that term, for its author, is incomparably richer and more shaded than can be grasped by the chance interviewer . . ." The word, so puritanically technical, stuck in my mind. It made me want to talk again with Jean Piaget . . . about Jean Piaget.)

Bringuier: Have you always been an unbeliever?

Piaget: Yes . . . No, not during my adolescence.

Bringuier: Did you have a religious crisis?

Piaget: No, because I promptly began to believe in immanence.

Bringuier: Captured by the love of knowledge.

Piaget: Knowledge indivisible from life.

Bringuier: Don't you ever miss having what they call "vertical" feelings?

Piaget: No, because to believe in the subject is to believe in the spirit. In that sense, I still believe in immanence.

Bringuier: One who believes in the spirit doesn't need to believe in God?

Piaget: No, and he certainly doesn't need an articulated system of metaphysics.

Bringuier: But isn't metaphysics, like the religious turn of mind or mysticism, a sign of one's longing for unity? That's what I meant about philosophy. One can't turn up one's nose at it too quickly, because the need exists. Man has a need for unity.

Piaget: But, to me, the search for unity is much more substantial than the affirmation of unity; the need and the search, and the idea that one is working at it . . .

Bringuier: That's what scientfic research is?

Piaget: Look: psychology, my field, tries to explain the whole man in his unity and not in the atomization of his behavior. Every study of children—of intelligence, perception, any subject at all—contributes to the picture of the whole. I don't see why this isn't searching for unity. It's just that science moves laboriously along, step by step, and with all sorts of controls. Well, it goes a good bit slower than building a system does.

Bringuier: And it's less spectacular.

Piaget: It's less spectacular. Now, the kind of system you're speaking of reaches unity very quickly, with a few years of reflection; but it's the unity of a certain individual who believes in his system. If someone doesn't believe in it, it isn't unity! For *he* has another system, and that already makes two. But science is a collective work, one in which scholars from every country add their bits to something that is the unity of worldwide psychological research—to take just one example.

Bringuier: You say that psychology accounts for, or tries to account for, the whole man?

Piaget: Yes. Freud said that no subject is taboo in psychology.

Bringuier: Still, to hear you talk about affectivity, for instance, one would think it was one of psychology's poor relations, in the sense that it becomes simply a motivating force.

Piaget: Why, not at all! I think it's a problem that's beyond us today. In fifty years we'll be able to talk about it intelligently, because it's considerably more difficult, and we don't have the neurological data. But, to use your terminology, scientific research is itself a search for unity: it daily affirms the strength of man's spirit.

Bringuier: Ah, well . . . we've been talking for a few minutes—too long for you—and I have the feeling that the man before me is sheltered by his profession, his work. You don't seem to be exposed to the world. Am I wrong?

Piaget: No, you're quite right. You can make life's little irritations disappear by burying yourself in your work.

Bringuier: I hope you'll forgive me for saying so, but there don't seem to be many irritations in your life.

Piaget: That's possible. Still, I was one of the most criticized of scholars, and my early works were harshly attacked, especially in the United States. I think it was Anthony, the psychiatrist, who wrote, "Piaget is much too narcissistic to have reacted to the criticism and has gone peacefully along in his own way."

Bringuier: Was he right?

Piaget: Yes. The other day a group of American psychologists sent me a *Festschrift,* and it contained a comment that pleased me very much. It was that for forty years I had completely scorned the ideas around me, the *Zeitgeist,* popular trends . . .

Bringuier: Which were in the air, yes.

Piaget: And—so said this kind scholar—as a consequence, now that I've been discovered, I'm not an ancestor but a contemporary—am even in the avant-garde. Of course, I was oblivious to trends for years, for I really read very little.

Bringuier: Yes, from that point of view, you work alone. Perhaps less so now?

Piaget: From that point of view. But I've always needed to work in a group.

Bringuier: Yes, but the group itself was an island, wasn't it?

Piaget: Yes, you're right.

Bringuier: I see that you wear your Legion of Honor pin. It's French . . .

Piaget: Yes, it's very useful.

Bringuier: Why?

Piaget: For customs, even for restaurants.

Bringuier: But you don't go through customs every day!

Piaget: Yes, I do—almost! The border is just ten minutes away from here by bicycle. Salève is in France, so practically every time I take a ride . . . Sometimes I'll be dripping with rain when I go into a pub over in Savoy; the fellow comes to chase me out, and then, when he sees the rosette, he finds me a seat. And customs officials, especially, give you less trouble.

Bringuier: I was just wondering if you were flattered by the honors you've received.

Piaget: Oh, they're always nice, but I wouldn't say I give them much thought. I'm delighted by the latest doctorate because it's the twentieth. I never thought I'd have twenty!

Bringuier: Next October?

Piaget: Yes.

Bringuier: Where?

Piaget: At Loyola University in Chicago. That way, I'll have the medal from the University of Moscow and the doctorate from the Jesuits!

Bringuier: What eclecticism! *(Laughter.)* Now you're almost universally recognized!

Piaget: Recognition, you know . . . *(Silence.)* I'm pleased by it, of course, but it's pretty catastrophic when I see how I'm understood.

Bringuier: Do you feel you've been badly interpreted?

Piaget: Yes, in general.

Bringuier: As to pedagogical application, or as to understanding of your research?

Piaget: No, no. As to understanding the theory itself. Well, I think it's the common lot. My colleagues understand it thoroughly. Besides, one keeps thinking one will be better understood later on.

Bringuier: Do you think in your case it's appropriate to speak of—and here's a word you surely won't like!—a passion for research?

Piaget: Oh, yes. Definitely. Very definitely.

Bringuier: Can you say anything about it? How does it work?

Piaget: Well, it's pretty hard to analyze. Finding a solid fact fills one with joy.

Part 1

Causality, or How Do We Interpret the Phenomena of the World?

We were to meet the following Saturday in the garden, after his weekly bicycle ride.

Bringuier: Did you have a good ride, M. Piaget?

Piaget: Excellent.

Bringuier: Did you go far?

Piaget: I went to the Filinger Bridge. It's behind Voirons, below the Pointe des Brasses. Oh, it isn't very far!

Bringuier: Ten or twelve kilometers?

Piaget: About.

Bringuier: Are these your plants here, in this corner of the garden?

Piaget: Yes, some of them. The ones that freeze in the winter I keep in the study, but these can stand the cold. The one from Vladivostok, for example, can certainly survive a winter in Geneva.

Bringuier: And what about that one, over there?

Piaget: That's from the south of France, from the mountains. This one is from the Rocky Mountains.

Bringuier: Have people brought them to you?

Piaget: No, some come as trades, some come from the Botanical Garden at Cornell University. Specialists are rare, but when you find one, he generally has a great many things. *(He stoops down, throws something.)* A snail!

Bringuier: Are they bad for the plants?

Piaget: Pretty bad. They'll eat them.

Bringuier: Where does this plant come from?

Piaget: Bulgaria. The one with the white flower comes from the banks of the Delaware. That one over there is from the mountains, near Zermatt. This one is from Asia. The one with yellow flowers . . . oh, that's a good story. I found it on a restaurant table in Berkeley, California, at a farewell dinner after some lectures. The table had been decorated with tiny sprigs of this sedum.

Bringuier: And you asked what it was?

Piaget: I carried them all away with me . . . no, I knew the species.

Bringuier: And you're still doing experiments with them on the fall of . . .

Piaget: Yes, on the fall of the secondary branches. It's a morphogenetic anticipation. But they aren't inherited structures—or at least they are so only in part. To a large degree, I think, it's a question of transfer, a question of adaptation during growth—epigenetic structure, as they say, and not hereditary only.

Bringuier: Do you come into the garden mainly for that?

Piaget: Well . . . yes.

> *(The conversation dies. I sense that he is inattentive and impatient.)*

Bringuier: Well, see you tomorrow?

Piaget: Tomorrow's fine, thank you.

Bringuier: I don't want to keep you any longer.

Piaget: Thanks very much. You must excuse me for the moment, but I've got a lot of work to do.

*He has scarcely any personal needs, other than
for a modest amount of tobacco. On that day
he had run short, and I offered him some of
mine.*

Bringuier: What do you think of it?

Piaget: It's not very strong.

Bringuier: Where does yours come from?

Piaget: Kentucky, I think. But it's prepared in Switzerland. I get it in Valais.

Bringuier: Do you smoke a lot?

Piaget: About twelve grams a day. I try to cut down, to please my doctor, though he doesn't see anything to be alarmed about.

Bringuier: I'm afraid that our conversations are a burden to you because they take you away from your work. I often feel that you're pressed for time, that you just don't have the time.

Piaget: Sometimes, yes. When we worked on causality, I felt it had to be done quickly. Now that it's coming into focus, I don't feel that as much.[1]

Bringuier: But generally, I think you ignore everything that might get in your way.

Piaget: It's certainly a shortcoming!

Bringuier: Is it true?

Piaget: Yes, I've always been like that.

Bringuier: In everything?

Piaget: If one wants to work, there have to be priorities. In *Le Temps retrouvé*, Proust writes a fine passage about it: at a time when he has only a little while remaining in which to finish his

---

1. For Piaget, like other writers perhaps, there are crises, tensions, and relaxations of time that would be interesting to study. There is a temporal topology, the route the writer-warrior follows. Causality presented this type of crisis, or obstacle, for Piaget. Claude Lévi-Strauss mentioned to me once in conversation that he, too, had somewhat similar experiences during the eight years it took him to complete and correct his *Mythologiques;* he abridged and tightened his discussions for fear of never finishing, of being submerged "till the end of time" by the masses of detail in the myths he was analyzing.

work, he reflects on the choice between the need to work and the services one could render right and left—relatively secondary, because others could do them—whereas what one undertakes oneself can be done by no one else . . . at least the idea one has . . .

Bringuier: Yesterday, when you came back from your ride, you weren't happy to see me, you had some things on your mind.

Piaget: That's true! I had to put them on paper before they vanished. It was the connection between two chapters that seemed to contradict each other.

Bringuier: In the book you're working on now?

Piaget: Yes. The work in progress, on causality. It isn't easy; no, it isn't easy.

Bringuier: How many chapters does it have now?

Piaget: Ninety-three. I finished it this morning. They aren't chapters for just one book. There are ninety-three investigations in draft form, from which I shall later write books.

Bringuier: They'll be divided into books.

Piaget: Yes. And then, in the field of causality, the possibility for contradiction is much greater than in the field of internal logicoarithmetical operations, because, with operations, the subject creates, constructs; whereas, with causality, it's the world of phenomena and objects. So, when you are changing from one experimental situation to another, you can get results that appear contradictory until you understand what isn't contradictory and why it nevertheless seems so. Well, yesterday, when I finished my ride, I was at that point.

Bringuier: So, you're working on causality now; or, rather, you're working on it again, for you pursued an investigation on the subject once before, I believe.

Piaget: Yes, in 1928 or 1930. But the problem was poorly stated. Now I've come back to it.

Bringuier: Almost fifty years later?

Piaget: Why, yes. And we've been at it for four years. It's a terrible problem!

Bringuier: How do you mean, terrible?

(A silence. He puffs on his pipe, then begins.)

Piaget: How does science explain phenomena? First of all, is the need for explanation fundamental? Or, as the positivists believe, does science simply describe . . . establish laws? With Meyerson and many others, I believe it's the need for explanation that's fundamental. Without that, there is no knowledge of the physical world. So, what is causality? What are explanatory procedures?

Bringuier: Here again, are you trying to break ground by experimenting with children?

Piaget: Yes, of course.

Bringuier: And why now?

Piaget: Listen. First, we studied the logic of the child. That was essential for the study of intelligence. Later we studied number, space, time, speed, and so forth. All this took years and resulted in a whole series of studies and books, but these are all operations of the subject. Then we realized, gradually, that the operations are easier when applied to one field than when applied to another, because, after all, there is the resistance of the object. So . . . what is the object for the subject? How can he explain the object's reactions? The problem of causality became logically imperative as a sequel to the study of the operations of the subject.

Bringuier: What kinds of experiments did you use?

Piaget: First, let's look at the general hypothesis. I think explanation always comes down to attributing to objects actions or operations analogous to our own, to the subject's—for instance, transmission, putting things together, displacement, etc. So causality would be a kind of attribution of our operations to objects, conceived as operators acting upon one another.

Bringuier: Is it magic?

(Surprised, he smiles.)

Piaget: No. Why in the world do you say that? All of microphysics uses operators that are copied from algebraic operators.

Bringuier: I mean, attributing to objects properties that seem in reality to be ours.

Piaget: It isn't attributing properties, it's thinking that objects behave rationally and act upon one another according to structures that are isomorphs of our mathematical operations. If they didn't, we wouldn't understand them. It isn't magic, it's the basic tenet of Western science.

Bringuier: Isomorphs . . . copied from?

Piaget: Yes, they're analogous. And when the child progresses in the representation he makes of the world around him, that is, when he acquires new structures, he begins to understand things that, until then, completely escaped him. Take, for example, the transmission of movement we spoke of before.

Bringuier: One marble hits another?

Piaget: If you like; but mainly it strikes the first one of a row of standing marbles, and the last one breaks away. We have to understand why it's the last one that moves. Now, for little children—four- and five-year-olds—the first marble came up to here, then it went behind and finally touched the one that rolled away; you couldn't see it, but that's what must have happened. All right. Then, around age six, the moving marble taps the first standing marble, which taps the second, which taps the last one, which breaks away. Each one taps the next one. That's still what the seven-year-old thinks, but, in addition, he has the idea that a little current goes through them, a shock.

Bringuier: A force . . .

Piaget: Yes, a shock, a force, which passes from one to the next—which goes through them. He still thinks the intermediate ones move slightly. And then, finally—not until he's about eleven—the child no longer needs to think that each one moves in order to animate the following one; it's the force of the first one that passes through all of them and is transmitted to the last one. We've come to the level of logical transitivity. If $A = B$ and $B = C$, then $A = C$. Applied to the object, it lets the child find invariants, as in mathematical operations. Here it's the conservation of movement. And the operations structured in the subject, at around eleven or twelve years of age, are what I call "formal" operations; they don't bear directly on the object but on possibility and hypotheses.

Bringuier: Formal as opposed to concrete?

Piaget: Yes, the child doesn't need to think that the intermediate marbles are displaced. A force can exist even when it can't be seen. This is an example of our research on causality, but at present we're at number ninety-three . . . before we manage to publish it . . . But each of my collaborators did one of the ninety-three studies, with students. It gives the students some training at the same time.

Bringuier: You haven't mentioned the work you did on causality forty years ago.

Piaget: Oh, yes, it was very bad. I was young.

Bringuier: In what way bad?

Piaget: Two or three things can be said about it—the explanation of the bicycle mechanism and things like that; but we failed to see a host of problems. Transmission itself. Especially the problem of vectors, directions. How are forces given direction? I'll describe an experiment to you I've just written up. The child is given a U-shaped tube filled with water, and one more drop of water is added at one end of the tube. Then a plunger, inserted into that end of the tube, is used to exert pressure, forcing the water up into the other arm. The child is then asked to say what the added drop is going to do. The little ones don't have any problem with it: it goes through the tube and comes out on the other side. It takes a long time before they understand that when the plunger presses on it, it can be only slightly displaced, because it is a part of the surrounding drops, and the first layer will press against the second and so forth. When they're at the level of believing that the drop passes through the tube, they have no idea about the direction of forces; they imagine liquid to be made up of elements that can escape in all directions, go off anywhere, overtake one another, and so forth. The whole problem of vectorial space, which gave us no end of trouble . . .

Bringuier: Do you take up old topics this way very often?

Piaget: Yes, yes—and how! We spend our time taking up old topics. It's never finished, is it?

What's absolutely astonishing is that we now have four hundred students and some sixty to eighty assistants, and there's enough work for everyone. It's always on problems of the development of intellectual structures. Each solution raises new problems and opens up new perspectives.

Bringuier: After causality, for example?

Piaget: Oh, the theory has a hole in it; we still don't have a clear view of the processes of equilibration.

Bringuier: . . . ?

Piaget: I think that, in addition to developmental factors—heredity or the maturation of the nervous system, external physical experience, the social milieu, language, and so forth—equilibration, we've mentioned it before, plays a major role: the fact that the subject tries to give the maximum degree of coherence to his ideas and to resolve contradictions. Seen this way, equilibration is an essential agent of development, but it must be studied again from this point of view. The theory isn't perfect yet. I expect that's what we'll do after causality.[2]

Bringuier: Somewhere—I can't remember where—you told of

2. *L'Equilibration des structures cognitives* was published in 1974 by Presses universitaires de France.

the scientist who begins to doubt his theory when it applies to every case. Were you just being clever?

Piaget: No. When you have a theory that can be applied too easily, you can suspect that it's too general and that it therefore doesn't explain very much.

Bringuier: Because the facts go right through it?

Piaget: Yes, the facts go right through it. If the facts don't offer any resistance, you can't be sure of the theory.

Bringuier: Basically, you're reassured when you find it in contradiction with the facts?

Piaget: No, not contradiction, but when you have difficulty fitting the facts to the theory.

Bringuier: I'd like to go back to the work on causality and to your original hypothesis. You say that the operations of the subject, when attributed to the objects themselves, are used by the subject to explain phenomena.

Piaget: That's right. In their actions, interactions, and reciprocal actions.

Bringuier: Now I'd like to ask you—but maybe this is too minor a point, too simple—if it's *true*. I mean, do objects really possess the properties we attribute to them?

Piaget: An object is a limit, mathematically speaking; we are constantly moving toward objectivity, we never attain the object itself. The object we believe we can attain is always the object as represented and interpreted by the intelligence of the subject.

Bringuier: Isn't that idealism?

Piaget: No, because the object exists. The object exists, but you can discover its properties only by successive approximations. It's the contrary of idealism. You are always getting closer but you never attain it, because, in order to attain it, you would necessarily have to grasp an infinite number of properties, but a great many of them escape you.

It's so far from idealism that I'll tell you a little story. Once we

extended an invitation to a specialist in mathematics, in
mathematical epistemology, from East Berlin. Well, she told me
that before she could come to Geneva and get her visa, she
would have to prove she had been invited by a materialist. So I
said to her, "Ah, very good, and who is the materialist you've
found in Geneva?" She said, "Why, you are!" I expressed some
surprise.

Bringuier: I can believe it.

Piaget: Wait. I said, "Who, me—a materialist?" "Why, yes:
you believe, as I do, that the object exists; and you believe, as I
do, that it can never be attained because it is only a mathematical
limit." I told her, "Yes, yes, if that's what materialism is, I agree
with you."

Bringuier: But you were still surprised?

Piaget: About what?

Bringuier: That she called you a materialist.

Piaget: When people say "materialist" without further elaboration, it always evokes naive materialism, the belief that
knowledge is only a copy of the world. But, for her as for me, it's
quite the contrary of a copy of the world; it's a reconstitution of
reality by the concepts of the subject, who, progressively and
with all kinds of experimental probes, approaches the object
without ever attaining it in itself.

Bringuier: Endlessly coming closer.

Piaget: Endlessly, limit . . .

Bringuier: Basically, you're more or less answering the old
question of whether, for instance, mathematics is in nature or in
the human mind.

Piaget: The choices you offer really surprise me. As a biologist, I think of the human mind as an essential part of nature. I
would put the question in another way: Does mathematics exist
in nature, including the human mind, or does it exist outside
nature . . . and then you have Platonism? In the latter case, mathematics is the set of possibilities, and the real, including the
human mind, is a tiny portion, infinitely small with respect to the

infinity of possibilities. But for me, mathematics exists in nature, and nature encompasses the human mind; the human mind develops mathematics with the body, the nervous system, and all the surrounding organism, which, itself, belongs to physical nature, in such a way that there is harmony between mathematics and the real world through the organism, and not through physical experience bearing on objects.

Bringuier: Then a person is compromised from the start.

Piaget: A person is compromised from the start. The human mind is a product of biological organization—a refined and superior product, granted, but still a product, like any other.

Part 2

*The Boss and the Team
(Three Conversations
at the International Center
for Genetic Epistemology)*

Piaget doesn't work alone, as he himself has said. At the Center for Genetic Epistemology, where his courses are given, Piaget, professor and director of research, has organized a working group of assistants, students, and scholars who collaborate with him in his studies while pursuing their own research projects. The atmosphere of the group, the way the studies are pursued, and the very originality of the undertaking seem to us to warrant including our conversations with these enthusiastic participants. This, too, is part of Piaget's life-work.

Howard Gruber is young, smiling, and white-haired. He wears a hippie-style shirt and an Indian necklace. He speaks French with a marked accent and many grammatical mistakes.

Bringuier: Howard Gruber, won't you introduce yourself?

Gruber: I'm a professor at Rutgers University. In French they say, "Rutgerse." It's the state university of New Jersey, close to New York. I teach courses in psychology, and I'm engaged in research.

Bringuier: That would be research in experimental psychology?

Gruber: That's right, and I'm also doing a study of creative thinking, based on the history of science and the lives of some major scholars—Charles Darwin, in particular.[1] Now I'm preparing a similar one on Jean Piaget.

Bringuier: It was this study that prompted your interest in him?

Gruber: If you consider creative thinking as a development that takes a long time and brings forth new ideas, it is very similar to the process of the child constructing his world, his thoughts, and his ideas, because the child does not learn simply what the adult tells him, he reinvents. It's a kind of creativity. Piaget is the psychologist who has done the most to develop a theory of creativity.

Bringuier: What's more, he's a creator himself.

Gruber: Of course.

Bringuier: I mean, it should be interesting for you from both points of view.

Gruber: Certainly. I talk with him, I look through the Piaget archives. I talk with his team—I'm a member of the team, in a way, I hope.

Bringuier: You participated with the team when they did the study on physical causality. That took him several years. It was a subject he'd worked on before, long ago. It seems to be characteristic of him, to go back.

Gruber: What's characteristic is that he's always looking for a

1. See Howard Gruber and Paul Barrett, *Darwin on Man: A Study of Scientific Creativity* (New York: Dutton, 1974).

synthesis of the whole. The synthesis moves ahead and becomes richer. So what he has already done must be done again. From time to time he returns to old problems. Causality is a good example. It's useful for him and for everyone, I think, because most psychologists don't have, well, the patience, the honesty, to throw themselves into a subject again.

Bringuier: And, maybe, the courage. You need that, in order to change.

Gruber: Yes. Specifically, it's important to think about the process by which a person rejects work he's already done. You do something. You publish the results. If they are really new, everyone will be critical. And they're right to criticize. Still, you have a certain need to be convincing. There's no doubt that Piaget is human and has the same need. In fact, some of the critics are right. Just listening to them carefully, without rejecting them out of hand, takes a kind of courage. But afterwards, in order to redo the work you had already done, abandon the ideas—which were good ideas, but simply outdated—that isn't easy. Even then, it isn't a question simply of rejecting some ideas and replacing them with others: the whole thing is done again. To build something new, really, one must neither abandon what one did nor become too fond of it. It has to be taken as something that can be rebuilt. I believe one of the most important strategies for great creative thinkers is having several things going on at once. Going on, I mean, for years.

Bringuier: Several parallel studies.

Gruber: That's right, exactly. A little bit independent of one another.

Bringuier: But related.

Gruber: Related, but each with its own characteristics, each moving in its own direction; and from time to time one tries to make a synthesis. Then, suddenly, one sees the link between two things. That's when you have the real construction. But to have several undertakings active at the same time, you have to work. Each one has to be done well, with its own strengths and with the promise of good results. Such work isn't carried on by a single individual. It takes a team. It's very much in Piaget's character to work with a team. Of course, he's the leader, the boss, and it's one of his fantastic talents that he's able to organize work for other people. But he's very democratic, too; he listens closely to the assistants, to his colleagues, and accepts their suggestions. It's possible to offer criticism, even harsh criticism.

Bringuier: He takes it into account.

Gruber: Yes, he takes it into account. He has a talent for listening carefully; if you think about what he did with children, it was thanks to the great respect he has for what they say. Everyone listens to children because they say such sweet things.

Bringuier: Yes, touching or amusing things.

Gruber: Amusing. But Piaget respects the child. He genuinely wants to understand the child for what he is.

Bringuier: The child is a person.

Gruber: Exactly: the child is a person. He must be understood. To do that, there must be respect. Piaget has a great deal of respect.

Bringuier: It's a kind of courtesy.

Gruber: It's more than that. Far more than that! A child has to make his way, find his own mind, just as a great thinker does, or the man in the street. It takes an effort to construct even a very ordinary idea, and a person feels joyful when he's done it. The child has the same feeling as the great thinker; it's a new and joyous discovery when you find it for the first time. In this sense, there is no such thing as banality, and a person can be happy spending his time with a child just because he is what he is.

Bringuier: I'd like to go back to your comments about studies conducted simultaneously and the links that are discovered between them. Doesn't this amount to a search for unity, when all is said and done?

Gruber: Yes, unity, or harmony. We think of science as discovering what there is in the world, but this isn't exactly true.

Science is a construction of the world through man's mind. What one is looking for is a construction that is beautiful, simple, and harmonious. Sometimes scholars speak of "beauty." They think an idea or a theory is "beautiful," not simply new. In this sense, science has much in common with art. Picasso has said that a picture is a sum of destructions: you paint, you erase, you paint, you erase, and you paint. You stop, not because you've finished—the task is never done—but because you've done your best, for the moment, and maybe, years later, you go back to the same picture and repaint it. You erase and you repaint...But still, you like what you've done. What you've done has beauty in it. Piaget has been applauded by the world for what he's done. Still, he has to erase. And do it over again. In order to do that, you have to have an idea of the total work. One has to look in one's mirror, and that, too, requires courage, having an idea of oneself that is pretty clear and complete. Do you understand?

I remember standing, one June morning, in the main symposium hall, which overlooks the lake, where the water sparkled in the sunlight. There, gathered around Jean Piaget for the regular annual week of work, were scholars from every country and every discipline. Among them were two young men, warm and friendly, hardly more than students.

After the meeting, we met in the "downstairs café," which serves as annex to the Faculté des Sciences. Guy Cellerier has since become codirector of the Center for Genetic Epistemology; Rafel Carreras teaches advanced physics to children and anyone else who wants to come.

Bringuier: I'd like you both to tell me how you happened to come to Piaget.

Carreras: You might say I came in here like a parachutist! I
had been in physics at l'Ecole Polytechnique in Zurich and
wanted to complement that work with a degree in biology,
which, at that time, included psychology. I think it still does.
I went to the psychology course Professor Piaget taught. I understood nothing at all and had the impression of being lost in a world
that was beyond me—one that I completely failed to grasp. I
thought I was wasting my time, so I stopped going to the course.
Still, for the exams, I worked terribly hard on Piaget. A few days before the exams I became really enthusiastic about his work. In the
written exam I wandered off the subject and went into a discussion
of intelligence in men from Mars; I talked about what the Martians'
intelligence might be. I thought sure I'd failed, but he gave me a
good grade—in fact, it was the highest. I went to see him and
said, "This is the kind of thing I'm interested in." He said,
"Come on Mondays." So I went on Monday—that was almost
six years ago—and gradually learned that Monday was the
meeting day for the Center for Genetic Epistemology. I've been
here ever since.

Bringuier: Guy Cellerier, do you also come on Monday?

Cellerier: I come on Monday. But I made a much longer de-
tour to get here than Carreras did. I was writing a thesis on the
foundation of international public law—which can be considered
an epistemological problem. I saw it as an epistemological problem.
I was reading Kelsen, the great philosopher of twentieth-century
law, and he quoted Piaget. In his biography . . .

Bringuier: And you didn't know who he was?

Cellerier: No, I didn't. Well, the name was vaguely familiar,
that's all. So I went to hear him. And I took a degree in biology,
then a doctorate in psychology with him.

Bringuier: And now?

Cellerier: Oh . . . I'm in cybernetics. I spent a year in the United
States studying the theory of automatons. Basically, I'm trying
to translate Piaget in terms of program simulation, into something
that would be programmable on a machine. But it all comes
from the intuitions he himself had, as a biologist, in 1920.

Bringuier: Please explain.

Cellerier: It appears that Piaget began working very early, around 1920, on what were basically precybernetic ideas. He considered an organism, the human being, acting in an environment, and he defined intelligence as that faculty of adaptation, that adaptation function, the ensemble of systems, leading to those adaptations. Well, that's exactly what cybernetics does now; as you know, there is a problem of construction in biology, the construction of an organism. At the beginning, embryological development, the organism, isn't complete. It isn't an animalcule with all its functions and all its organs ready-made and just waiting to grow. It's a construction, just like what happens in a factory when you build a car.

Bringuier: In the fetus?

Cellerier: Yes, in the fetus. There is a plan for building the machine; you build the motor . . . no, that's not a very good comparison; but still, it's the realization of a design. That's the important thing. The design is realized progressively, and the structures that are constructed, or the parts, the organs, that are constructed, start to interact and are built by interaction with each other.

Bringuier: The design is the genetic system?

Cellerier: That's right. It's the genetic program. In short, for Piaget—this is my interpretation—embryogenetic development is the model of the development of mental faculties.

Bringuier: But what's the relation to cybernetics? You began by saying . . .

Cellerier: That's just the way cyberneticians attack problems now! In both cases you have a process of the flow of information. The modern description of the development of embryogenesis basically describes an automaton. It all happens exactly as it would in a computer with a preset program. It follows the program. So, in that sense, you can see embryogenesis, life, as an information-flow machine, in opposition to the energy-flow machines that physicists study. Well, people who study artificial intelligence consider thought this way: the subject is also an information-flow machine; thought consists of manipulating symbols. According to rules. In both cases, you have information-flow machines, and in both cases we're trying to find out the rules that govern the production of the flow.

Bringuier: But how are the rules comparable?

Cellerier: I won't say they're perfectly comparable. I don't agree with Piaget on this point. I think the embryogenetic program is infinitely stupider than the human brain.

Bringuier: The individual?

Gruber: No, the group, the genetic pool! In evolution, the individual is the species itself, the ensemble of all the genes that combine, and the genetic program is the result of calculations made by this enormous system. I personally would like Piaget to replace "epigenesis"—development of the embryo—by "genetic system." That would be wonderful!

Bringuier: You should tell him.

Cellerier: I have. I even wrote a thesis telling him about it. The upshot is we've agreed to disagree. But the fact remains that taking two things as dissimilar as the genetic system and human thought and suggesting that they have something in common, and to do it in 1920, was a stroke of genius. It's still revolutionary.

Carreras: Because, fundamentally, the genetic system solves problems. When the species confronts a changing environment, for example, the genetic system solves the problem of adaptation. That's why there is a magnificent continuity between Piaget and this approach, because Piaget defined human intelligence as a system adapting to a changing environment.

Cellerier: What has to be done now is to translate this approach, which was biological and in a sense purely intuitive, into formal systems acceptable to people working with artificial intelligence. In the United States, Piaget is ultramodern because engineers are discovering that Piaget asked these very questions forty years before them.

Bringuier: Relative to the child?

Cellerier: Relative to the child. Relative to a natural system being programmed in the course of his education.

Bringuier: Rafel Carreras, what do you do at the Center?

Carreras: Well, as a physicist, my main role is to explain certain problems in physics that deal with epistemology, as well as to get ideas for the experiments, give explanations, sometimes ridiculous ones, but making it easier sometimes for the others to have ideas.

Bringuier: When you say "the others" . . . ?

Carreras: I mean the people who come on Monday, or guests in all the disciplines. Cellerier was just talking about cybernetics, but we have ecologists, biologists, logicians, physicists—you could say scientists of every stripe, because some specialize in areas that touch on two or three other disciplines.

Bringuier: The people who are here are open to a variety of things.

Carreras: They're open. Yes. If a person is closed, he'll be completely lost. At first, that's what happens to everyone, and here, with Piaget, there's a kind of crisis—each of us has described his own; and when you have famous people, it may be even harder for them to accept the fact that they suddenly fail to understand anything for a while. You have to have a certain flexibility, understand a variety of points of view, and especially, their expression in different languages—the vocabulary, the meaning of words—"causality," for example. These are very different for a biologist, a logician, and a physicist.

Cellerier: They're concepts belonging to very different categories. We have to try to be more flexible in our thinking.

Carreras: Everyone tries to understand what the other person means when he uses words that are sometimes the same, and that's just what . . .

Cellerier: Still, the discussions are kept within bounds by the fact that there is a central topic. This year, it's causality. People's thinking is channeled toward that topic.

Bringuier: Each one talks about causality in terms of his own discipline?

Cellerier: That's right.

Bringuier: The physicist talks about causality with the meaning it has in physics; the biologist gives it a different meaning.

Carreras: Perhaps the most interesting thing is that when the physicist listens to the biologist, he gets ideas he perhaps hasn't had before. Then he suddenly interrupts the biologist with a comment. Now, three-fourths of the time his remarks are completely inappropriate, completely ridiculous; but once in a while they bridge the disciplines and offer some clarification. Then the biologist says, "Well, frankly, I'd never thought of that approach." And maybe just then a man in the history of science says, "Why, what you're suggesting is what a certain person tried centuries ago. A Descartes, or an Aristotle, or an Archimedes had already started out in that direction." Then and there, Piaget, who leads his group without saying very much yet more or less directs everyone, says, "Mr. So-and-so, you'll give us a little talk on that person two weeks from now." Naturally, you're glad you were there.

Cellerier: In short, you might say that Piaget hasn't mastered all the disciplines because it's not humanly possible.

Carreras: But perhaps in compensation—because he's not buried in problems that are too technical—he can concentrate on his trajectories—the epistemological aspect, so to speak; he goes below the surface, gets rid of all the technical "red tape," pares it down. I don't know how to put it in French—you have the impression he goes directly to the heart of the matter.

Cellerier: He returns to the central problems. For him, these are knowledge and the acquisition of knowledge. If you get lost in detail during your comments, Piaget picks out the four or five essential ideas and puts you back on the track.

Carreras: From the beginning, he's focused on certain basic aspects of all the sciences he's studied. Something the scientist who specializes doesn't really have the chance to do.

Cellerier: He always observes the psychological subject. He isn't like certain mathematicians for whom, basically, the subject who does mathematics becomes a mathematical being himself, an abstract being. Piaget retains, he follows, a natural train of thought, behind his formal expressions. He keeps the subject in mind. Behind physics there is the physicist; behind mathematics, the mathematician. It's this common element that allows understanding to occur, that lets him move from one science to another.

Carreras: And if it's a question of biology or animal studies, clearly it's completely different from studying the magnetic field. But the brain that considers the animal, the thought that turns to the animal, and the thought that turns to the magnetic field, all have the same base. One can go back to the early years of life, to the instinct for conservation, the factors of classification, the operations—the basics are exactly the same. Sometimes in my "popular" classes I like to present modern physics and show how close it is, fundamentally, to what children do. What is done by the child of four, five, or six can often be described in the same words that describe what is done by absolutely contemporary physicists. The words are the same. They try to bring order out of chaos, and they use the same operations, the same classifications, to such a degree that it can seem—I won't say humiliating—but shocking. But you have to see that the basic mechanisms are the same. That's what hadn't perhaps been seen so clearly before Piaget. The hodgepodge you see in a group like ours is only a hodgepodge in appearance. All these different people have a certain number of experiences in common in the study of the growth of knowledge, and they manage to find a common ground in this idea, once they've clearly understood what they're talking about.

Cellerier: Take a topic like causality, for a physicist. Physicists are concerned with causality—even if they never want to hear the word, they think it's too "psychological"—because they will state, for instance, "Every time a certain thing happens . . . a certain other thing happens." With the cause implying, in a certain sense, the effect. So what can be done in a situation where we are blocked by a word? What, for instance, can the logician do? The logician will deal with the link between cause and effect, and he's going to wonder if the implicative links in logic correspond to any part of what physicists call the cause-and-effect relationship. To go back to cybernetics, the cybernetician asks himself, "What can causality be used for?" Causality *qua* category. In classical philosophy—take Kant—you have categories: time, space, and causality. What are they used for? They're present for the philosopher; but does a person who wants to build a robot, a sensory-motor robot that can move about, follow orders, and wash dishes, need such categories? No doubt he needs space for the robot to move in; he needs at least some of that category. And of course he needs time, because the actions must occur in a certain order. Does he need causality? Does he have to know things like . . . I'm thinking of a famous experiment: I lift up a one-kilogram object with the "normal" effort the act requires; then I lift up another object that is identical in appearance, but it weighs only a few grams, and my hand flies up too high.

Bringuier: Because you are surprised?

Cellerier: Because I didn't have the information about the properties of the material—just those causal properties of the material that cannot be reduced to geometrical properties. Think about the experiments performed with manipulators at M.I.T.

Bringuier: An eye and a hand?

Cellerier: Yes, an articulated hand and a TV camera connected by a computer. One difficulty we often saw was that when the hand wanted to grasp a glass, it grasped it as if it were made of steel—and the glass broke. Piaget has shown that these categories, which are in fact indispensable, are constructed. They aren't given a priori. Basically, the child learns space, time, and causality. He constructs it.

Bringuier: This is the process that constitutes the stages.

Cellerier: The famous stages. Piaget was fascinated by the construction of the Kantian categories. He reversed the philosopher's proposition. In Kant, the categories are present at the beginning, as given forms of human understanding. You can interpret the world only through structures established a priori. They're filters present in the machine from the outset. Piaget says the opposite.

He says the same thing as Kant, insofar as he, too, states that one can interpret the world only through these structures; but for him the structures are constructed at the time the subject interprets reality. To put it another way, there is an interaction between the external environment and what goes on inside the subject. I think all cyberneticians will agree on this point. So the structures are constructed, and only at the end do they have the quality of logical and absolute necessity that Kant attributed to them. It's one of Piaget's most profound ideas: the counterpart of an algebraic system, an example of a closed, complete state, the psychological counterpart of the mathematical structure, is the feeling of necessity—precisely the "resistance" of the structure. And necessity comes at the end.

But to go back to the example of discussions centering on a word: you can see the physicist or the cybernetician manipulating causality and being more or less aware of it, and that's what has to be made clear in what Carreras calls the "hodgepodge."

Bringuier: For you two, for all of you here, does "understand" mean "make understood"?

Carreras: No doubt; because one learns what one understands as one tries to communicate it. It's what happens when you do a tracing. That's an experiment everyone should try at least once in his life! Maybe during a vacation. You use a photograph—someone's picture, a good clear image—and over the photograph you a lay a very thin sheet of tracing paper. You take a sharp pencil and trace over it, following the main outlines. And you're pleased; you've done it, and it's good. It's good as long as you keep the photograph behind it. You remove the tracing paper and show it to someone. It's usually a disaster! Maybe you forgot to do the nose, the eyes—that can happen! When the tracing paper is very transparent, you forget where you've been. The result is a monstrosity.

That's what you're doing when you try to communicate. Within yourself you have a certain image, a set of expressions, your experience, and you try to trace it with words and pass it along. Often it's catastrophic.

Bringuier: What you pass on to the next person is the tracing.

Carreras: You pass on the tracing when you believe you've given the photograph. That's the story of the popularization of science—and of communication between individuals in general. You forget to define certain things that turn out to be the most important. The problem of Piaget is to start from what you have in your own head and reconstitute the flesh of the photograph. Complete the tracing. Fill in the missing parts.

Bringuier: But in his case, and with his own thoughts, does he give you tracings or photographs?

Carreras: I don't mean to be unkind, but sometimes I get the impression he gives us bits of the tracing! Perhaps it's difficult for him to make tracings, and probably it's not his job, not his calling. There are enough of us to help each other try to reconstitute it.

Cellerier: That's true, and I think it would be useful to say that Piaget thinks in very strong unities. He doesn't . . . make small change. He has ideas about the main problems, but he doesn't divide it up into sufficiently small units for the uninformed listener.

> *I met with Howard Gruber again. Guy Cellerier joined us during the conversation.*

Bringuier: Howard Gruber, you've alluded to the average man, to the "common" man. How is someone like Piaget different from other men who work?

Gruber: They have a lot in common, because, as I said, everyone has to create his world; at bottom, you might say, they're basically exactly alike. That's one of the reassuring things I've learned! The genius's memory is no different from the memory of the man in the street, but it's organized differently. It's precisely the organization of the system that is different.

And his life, let's say, is different. A creative man's life is much harder; he works a good deal more.

Piaget works all the time, all the time. That doesn't mean he doesn't play, because work, too, is a kind of play. But he has a goal. Piaget's goal is to construct the logic of the human mind, the logic of life, and to discover the genesis of the logic of life. It's a goal he's pursued for a long time. A goal that guides practically everything he does. The average man doesn't have a goal of this type. He responds much more to external demands, I think. Piaget also responds to the external world, but within the framework of his goal.

There is something else. The "common" man has his social world for his team. Piaget builds his team, and what he does is considerably more than any one person could do by himself. He works closely with his team. For other creative men, it's the same thing, even if the team isn't present in fact; bonds are developed with other scholars, and that's a kind of team, too. Contrary to the popular notion, the creative man has close links with the world; he needs the world in order to correct himself and to find new ideas. I think he's less alone than the average man.

Bringuier: You said, "Work is a kind of play."

Gruber: Yes. Piaget includes play with his work; play is always present in his work. When you arrive at the Center for Epistemology, Monday morning, you find an assistant who's been to X's—the big children's store in Geneva—and has found a plaything that he's fashioned an experiment from. He shows it around. I found this quality in Darwin too—not in the same way, because he worked on animals rather than children, but the same spirit of play penetrates everything, the most serious things.

Cellerier: I'm thinking about Gruber's comment on the goal, the basic project. There's an unbelievable unity in Piaget's thought. When you consider the texts he wrote at the age of thirteen and fourteen . . . in the novel, *Recherche*—published when he was twenty, I think—assimilation and equilibrium already appear. Later he used other models, he assimilated people in passing, he integrated new theories; but he has always kept to his own line of thought. One year you can talk to him about a problem of deep interest to you, and he says politely, "That's interesting," but the conversation will stop. If you talk to him about the same thing the next year, when it relates to his current interest, he'll say, "Here's what should be done, here's how to look at the problem." He perceives what crosses his path, what comes into his target area.

Bringuier: (To Gruber) You're an American. Wasn't he recognized pretty late in America?

Gruber: Yes, because in America we have the habit of mass production. This idea has been applied to psychology. The idea I emphasized before—that in order to build, one must destroy, that is, turn away from the investments one's made—it's costly, it's not economical. It's not the style. It's better to have a theory that can simply be added to. We Americans add all the time. It works, for *things!* I think that's the mistake we've made; the result isn't a fruitful psychology that explains how the child becomes himself, becomes what he is. Consequently, our recognition of Piaget came late. But now he is read extensively and cited frequently. I'm not sure that he's been completely understood; but at least he'll win his place. He receives honors from us, a heap of honors—like this! *(He gestures. Silence.)* It's not exactly the same thing as being understood.

Cellerier: Maybe I'm not well enough acquainted with American psychology, but I think many psychologists in fact understand him the wrong way. I think theoreticians, those working with artificial intelligence, understand him better. It's a paradox of his success in the United States: Piaget is spoken of more eloquently in computer-science departments than in psychology departments.

Bringuier: What's the result when Piaget is wrongly understood?

Cellerier: Well, everyone claims Piaget for himself or rejects him. For example, a psychologist—I can't remember his name—whom Piaget described at the symposium: "He wrote a book to prove that I am in fact a maturationist!"—that is, that intelligence is already programmed in the genetic inheritance, and that the stages of knowledge are only stages in the maturation of the organism.

Bringuier: All set in advance . . .

Cellerier: That's right. Everything programmed. There was another one who wrote a book about him saying, "No, no, Piaget is a new behaviorist, a neoassociationist." That's the kind of misunderstanding that occurs.

Gruber: I'd like to add something about the contradictions that seem to be present in the whole of a man's work. Some people find contradictions, and they cite this and that that don't go together—precise points. But when you are dealing with a major body of work, resting on the work of several decades, these are often changes in perspective rather than real contradictions. Take Darwin: it was necessary to have the idea of species in order to find the theory of evolution; but once that theory was found, the idea of the species got less attention. I don't mean that there are no real contradictions, but there is often something else to be discovered behind the apparent contradictions.

Bringuier: Tell, me, what was the state of psychology before Piaget?

Cellerier: I hardly know how to describe it. There was a kind of—what can I say?—unbelievable jumble. I'm always surprised when Piaget quotes De Saussure and Baldwin, the first ones; but when you read those men, you see that there's a mass, there was already a mass, of intuitions—scattered out, but basic. And then, afterwards, with Piaget, you have superb order. He imposed the structures. In a sense, almost everything was there already. Had been, ever since Dalton. Dalton's experiments are very much like Piaget's. He did them on himself, of course, but that wasn't the main thing.

Bringuier: He reorganized.

Cellerier: Yes. It's a sort of Einsteinian revolution in psychology, and maybe even more startling; because Newton was already someone whose thought was coherent, whereas that wasn't true of most psychologists. Psychology separated very slowly from philosophy; it didn't have the sort of requirements, or the demand for logical precision, that it now has.

Bringuier: Scientific.

Cellerier: Yes. Formal exactitude. That makes it all the more spectacular.

Bringuier: It's true that when you think of the word "psychology," you think of something that is vaguely philosophical rather than something scientific.

Cellerier: Psychology began to separate itself from philosophy, at least for me, only after Piaget, only with Piaget.

Taking Consciousness [La prise de conscience] *(1975–76)*

I visited Piaget again, six years later. He hadn't changed much. He was working even more, if that's possible. His eightieth birthday is being celebrated this year.

Bringuier: You haven't given up your pipe, I see.
Piaget: No.
Bringuier: The doctors haven't forbidden you to smoke?
Piaget: They're making me cut down.
Bringuier: You still smoke a meerschaum?
Piaget: Yes, always. There's nothing like it!

(Silence. We smoke for a while.)

Bringuier: I've just realized that I know nothing about your preferences in food. Do you enjoy eating?
Piaget: Very much! I like . . . *(Laughter. But he seems reluctant to talk about it. He does so out of pure courtesy.)* I like the fondue I make from my own recipe; that is, instead of putting in

a clove of garlic, I use a whole bulb, lots of kirsch, and lots of wine, and little bit of cheese as filler. You can drink half of it and eat the other half by soaking your bread in it.

Bringuier: Your wife makes it for you?

Piaget: No, she doesn't like it.

Bringuier: You do the cooking yourself?

Piaget: When we're in the mountains.

Bringuier: At the chalet?

Piaget: Yes.

> *(He goes there in the summer, but it is winter now.)*

Bringuier: Am I wrong, or have you put things in order here in the study in the past six years?

Piaget: I had to do it just once; it was unavoidable, because my writing table began to push me away.

Bringuier: On this side?

Piaget: Yes, on your side. I could no longer find a place for my paper. If I'm going to write, I have to have somewhere to write, and I cleaned my study after three days of complete depression.

Bringuier: What did you take away? Just the top part?

Piaget: Displacement. Straightening up a study—it's the way it is in philosophy, the problems are displaced.

Bringuier: Ah, so. And now you can find your way around?

Piaget: Generally speaking, yes. In my whole life I've lost only one paper. It was about the plants I'm still studying, the sedums, and I had written an article about them. Then I just couldn't locate it; I had to rewrite it. It's one of the rare instances when I am in complete agreement with Freud about lapses and errors in action. I certainly lost it on purpose; it wasn't good.

Bringuier: And what you rewrote was more satisfactory?

Piaget: Oh, yes, certainly.

Bringuier: Why do you say "one of the few times" you've agreed with Freud?

Piaget: I mean, agreed with Freud's interpretation of lapses, his interpretation of parapraxes. Because there are many that are automatic, and they don't all have unconscious reasons. But in this case there was quite clearly an intention. The article was bad, and I wouldn't have had the courage to burn it; so losing it was a solution.

Bringuier: Over and above lapses, can it be said that you generally agree with Freud?

Piaget: Oh, on the main lines of repression and the basic mechanisms of the unconscious, of course. But, in interpretations of detail, it's like a historical reconstitution. You're working with truth up to a certain level, a certain limit, beyond which the reconstruction is more or less arbitrary, and it's impossible to draw a line between the two.

Bringuier: I may be mistaken, but I don't think you've ever used his work. It's often said you've underestimated it or dismissed it.

Piaget: No, no, that's a basic misunderstanding. I shall answer this reproach about psychoanalysis just as I do for affectivity in general.

Bringuier: Yes, we've mentioned the role of affect, or rather, its absence, in your work.

Piaget: Well, I probably said then that affectivity is basic as a motive for action. If a person isn't interested in something, he won't do anything, of course; but it's only a motive, and it isn't the source of the structures of knowledge. Since my concern is with knowledge, I have no reason to consider problems of affect; but it isn't because of a disagreement but because of a distinction, a difference of interests. It isn't my domain. Generally speaking—and I'm ashamed to say it—I'm not really interested in individuals, in the individual. I'm interested in what is general in the development of intelligence and knowledge, whereas psychoanalysis is essentially an analysis of individual situations, individual problems, and so forth.

Bringuier: At bottom, human beings interest you less as individuals than as invariants?

Piaget: Yes, that's right, that's right. But psychoanalysis has always interested me. To give you an example, I lectured at the American Psychoanalytic Association, the largest Freudian association in the world, I think. I gave a lecture three or four years ago on the cognitive unconscious and the affective unconscious, to show the relationships. It was published in French in *Raison Présente.*

Bringuier: That is, between the unconscious touching on intelligence, and the unconscious touching on affectivity?

Piaget: Yes.

Bringuier: What can be said about it?

Piaget: One can say that a majority, a very great part, of the individual's activities in his cognitive work, in his search for solutions to problems, remains unconscious when the action succeeds, and that taking consciousness comes well after the action itself.

Bringuier: That is, taking consciousness doesn't occur as long as there is no need for it?

Piaget: That's right, exactly.

Bringuier: And in affectivity?

Piaget: Well, in affectivity, you have the same thing and also repression. But, for repression, you can also find plenty of analogies in the cognitive domain: when the individual—a child or sometimes even a scientist—constructs a concept or theory, especially a theory, he unconsciously represses what doesn't work.

Bringuier: He chooses what...

Piaget: Of course. There you have the cognitive equivalent of Freudian repression, and I emphasized this in the lecture.

Bringuier: One doesn't want to recognize what doesn't fit nicely into the system.

Piaget: That's right.

*With only a few words of conversation we had
come directly to the heart of his work. I knew
that "taking consciousness" belonged to the
area of his new undertakings. It was brought
up when he mentioned the lost article on
sedums, but no doubt any other opening
would have led him equally quickly to his central concerns. He was just as I remembered
him: absorbed by the work in progress, by the
part of his life's work in which he was engaged
at the moment, and by nothing else.*

Bringuier: Let's talk a bit about the studies you've done in the
past few years, since causality.

Piaget: At the Center for Genetic Epistemology we did a series
of studies on "taking consciousness," and I edited a little book
on it. One study was quite amusing. I'll tell you about it. We
asked children to crawl and then describe their movements. We
found three stages. The youngest ones gave us a ridiculous explanation: they told us that they moved their two hands forward,
then their two feet forward, then their hands, etc.—which is obviously impossible. At a second stage they said: I put the left arm
and the left leg forward, then the right arm and the right leg
forward—which is possible but unusual; even horses don't often
walk this way. Then the children in the third group described it
accurately.

Bringuier: With alternate diagonals.

Piaget: Yes, the left hand and the right foot, right hand and
left foot. So, before the annual symposium, when distinguished
guests from outside come for a discussion of the year's work,
the collaborator who had done this study had an excellent idea:
she would ask our distinguished guests to try the experiment,
and she had them walk on all fours.

Bringuier: In the symposium room?

Piaget: No, no, by themselves, so that the others wouldn't see them, you know—each one individually. She asked them to walk on all fours and describe the movements they made. The results were astonishing. The physicists and the psychologists gave accurate descriptions—they were at the third stage. But the logicians and mathematicians gave the second-level description, which isn't at all absurd; logically it's the simplest, but it isn't the way they'd walked at all. In other words, they had no consciousness of the movements they'd made and had reconstituted it conceptually. Taking consciousness is an accurate conceptualization in most cases, but it can give rise to distortions like this.

Bringuier: How do you explain the difference between the two groups?

Piaget: The two groups? Psychologists and physicists are accustomed to looking beyond themselves to the facts, whereas mathematicians reconstruct the model that seems simplest and most logical to them.

Bringuier: And they're mistaken.

Piaget: In this case they were mistaken. It demonstrates that there is no taking consciousness in an action that they had actually made, maybe not every day as adults, but pretty surely at one time. Our result on the theoretical level is that taking consciousness is far from being a simple beam of light like a flashlight, which would simply let us see what couldn't be seen before, but without transforming anything.

Bringuier: Letting one see what one had done.

Piaget: Yes, that's right. In fact, taking consciousness is a conceptual reconstitution of what the action did.

Bringuier: Well, isn't that the same thing?

Piaget: No, reconstitution means there is much more.

Bringuier: What more is there?

Piaget: There is the consciousness of connections, there is generalization, and so forth.

Bringuier: The relations between various moments of action . . .

Piaget: That's it. In other words, the action, alone, tends toward a goal, and it's satisfied when the goal is achieved. It is dominated by what I would call "success." Whereas taking consciousness also contains understanding: you know how you succeeded. My book on taking consciousness was too long—that often happens to me—so I made it into two, and the second one is called *Succeeding and Understanding*, but it's the same subject. Taking consciousness is the interpretation and explanation of the action. In the action itself, comprehension is focused on the object and not on the mechanisms that allowed it to be attained.

Bringuier: Is what you've called "reflection" useful too? I mean, does it prepare for something else, or is it satisfied with results?

Piaget: First, of course, it can produce new actions; because one opens up new possibilities when one has understood what one has done. Then again, as an explanatory model, it is the point of departure for a series of other conceptualizations.

Bringuier: The desire to repeat the same thing, or to repeat it with modification, etcetera.

Piaget: Yes, that's right. But with a much larger field of generalization.

*Games for Children and Scholars:
Toward a Comparative History
of Individual Intelligence and
Scientific Progress*

The succession of scholars is like a single man
endlessly learning.
Pascal

Bringuier: So, that belongs to the research you've been doing
for the past four or five years? When I last saw you, you were
working on causality.

Piaget: (He lights his pipe again.) Taking consciousness: we
went into that right after the causality studies. Causality being
the operations attributed to the object at the level at which the
child attains operations. But before that they're the actions of the
subject attributed to objects. Of course this raised the question of
the role of action in knowledge. We had to distinguish action
qua action, action properly so-called, from conceptualized
action.

Bringuier: So one study leads to another. In the study that's
nearly done you discover the studies yet to be done.

Piaget: Yes, it's step by step. But not necessarily in a straight
line. A study often opens up several others simultaneously. In
that case, you have to make a choice. We also take up topics

again—causality and equilibration are good examples—because sometimes, thank goodness, as the work progresses, it feeds, it enriches, former studies by contributing new facts or modifying the theory. Then we pull out the old file folders again. There's permanent interaction.

Then again, an idea ripens little by little on the periphery of the actual study. That can go on for years and years, and then, suddenly, it comes to be the topic for a study in its own right. Our reflections on the comparative development of intelligence in the child and in scientific progress are a case in point; right now, I'm writing a book on these similarities with a splendid colleague, a physicist, Rolando Garcia, former dean of the Faculty of Sciences in Buenos Aires.

Bringuier: Can we stop here for a moment? I'm glad you mentioned that. For you, seeing a child take shape intellectually and seeing the progress of mankind from prehistoric times to the present are nearly the same thing. What ground do you have for thinking that?

Piaget: Let me explain. I was interested in both biology and problems of knowledge in general. As a biologist, I wanted to understand how knowledge takes shape, what its genesis is, its mode of elaboration. And for that, prehistoric man would have been the ideal field of inquiry, as I've said before; but nothing, or practically nothing, is known about his mentality. So we had to do what they do in biology when the history of phylogenesis can't be reconstructed: you study ontogenesis, that is, individual development, which is clearly related to phylogenesis. Moreover, I believe, with Baldwin and with Freud as well, that the child is more primitive than *any* adult, including prehistoric man, and that the source of knowledge lies in ontogenesis. Any adult you choose, whether cave man or Aristotle, began as a child and for the rest of his life used the instruments he created in his earliest years. Consequently, in the field of knowledge—I'm not generalizing to every field—ontogenesis is basic. I would say that it's more primitive than phylogenesis.

Bringuier: Now I have a second question: Is today's child less primitive than the human child of prehistoric times?

Piaget: I have no idea. I suppose that, with civilization and the social environment, which can't help but play a significant role, there is an acceleration and that today's child evolves more rapidly.

Bringuier: Because of the social environment?

Piaget: Obviously! The environment prompts him and sets him any number of problems the primitive child never encountered. But to return to the main question: wherever one sees the beginnings of knowledge, one finds a process very similar to the process one sees in the child.

Bringuier: For example?

Piaget: An example, let's see . . . *(He puffs on his pipe and settles into his chair.)* For the early periods of science—that is, at a time when physics was just taking shape and wasn't what it's become since Newton—history shows stages that correspond astonishingly well to stages I've observed in children. Take the transmission of movement, for instance, which we studied in causality. How does movement pass from a moving object to another object when the first one touches the second? In the pre-Newtonian period—say, before the seventeenth century—we can distinguish roughly four periods.

There is the period of Aristotle and the theory of two movers: the agent is a motive force coming to collide with the passive one, that is, the ball that isn't moving, which also has its own force and internal mover. The transmission of the movement consists of the excitation of the internal mover of the second mover by the first. There is also the theory of the proper place; that is, each body tends toward a particular place—one that in some way appears to be intended for it.

Bringuier: All of this to explain the transmission of movement?

Piaget: Yes. When a projectile leaves the machine, why doesn't it fall straight down to the ground and continue on its way?

Aristotle proposed a theory that seemed very sophisticated, the *antiperistasis;* that is, the surrounding reaction, the mobile, is an air current flowing from behind to push it forward. That's the first period.

Second period, between Aristotle and Buridan: the internal mover is dropped; everything is attributed to the external mover. It has the power, the impulse, the force, the work—everything! Then, in the third period, with Buridan, you have the *impetus.* Something called the "impetus" acts between the cause and the effect, a force—the force provided by the external mover and transmitted to the receiver, the passive element. Then, in the fourth period, the impetus becomes acceleration, and we are on the eve of Newton.

While working on causality, we gave close attention to the transmission of movement in all its forms. We found these same four periods in the child.

Bringuier: Between what ages?

Piaget: Between the ages of four or five and eleven or twelve. So we have: first period, Aristotelian. Not only does the child speak of two movers in his own language—the ball that moves against the other one has force, the one receiving the shock also has force; the two forces cause them to move forward. The child talks about the "proper place," too. For example, a marble rolls down an inclined plane. Why does it roll? A seven-year-old told me, "It has to go back to its natural place." The natural place is exactly the same as the proper place. But what's even better is the *antiperistasis.* When you ask a child, "When you throw a ball, why does it keep going instead of falling?" he says, "When I throw it, I make a breeze that pushes it forward." That's actually *antiperistasis.* For children, it comes chiefly from the relation between clouds and wind: if the clouds move, it makes a little wind; if they move with greater force, it makes more wind; if they push even harder . . .

Bringuier: You have perpetual movement.

Piaget: Yes. That's the Aristotelian theory. Then the second stage: the internal mover no longer plays a role, and force becomes undifferentiated, a power copied from human activity. And then in the third period: impetus. When they're seven or eight years old, all children talk about force. The marble that collides with another gives it a force. When you have a series of marbles and the last one shoots out, it's because the force *passes through* the others, whereas younger children never tell you that. When they're eleven or twelve, they no longer speak of force but of acceleration: it rolls down the plane faster and faster.

Now this is for the early periods of science; but in the more advanced periods—take the history of geometry, for example, Garcia has written a very good chapter about it—you find what I call "common mechanisms." In geometry, the common mechanisms are these: in the first stage all the geometric spatial relations the child constructs are strictly intrafigural, just as for Euclid.

Bringuier: That is . . .

Piaget: That is, relations internal to the figure. There's no space between the figures. Euclid never made a general theory of space, only a theory of figures. The second stage is interfigural. It is the Cartesian coordinates: a point is a function of two coordinate axes; two measurements are required to fix the position of a point on a plane. The third step is the algebraization of geometry, starting with Klein and the Erlangen program; all geometries are reduced to displacement groups or transformation groups. Now that's a mechanism common to the history of science and psychogenesis. Among children, you have an intrafigural period, of course; and if you talk about what happens between figures and space, it doesn't exist. They really have no idea about it. When they're seven or eight years old, they make a discovery: when you want to determine the position of a point—if you want to put it in the same place on another piece of paper—you must have at least two measurements, two coordinates, you see, but in action. The child doesn't have a theory, but you find this in their action, and then, later, algebraization; that is, geometric relations begin to form systems. Again you have, in action, something more or less the equivalent of displacement groups, transformation groups. *(A silence.)*

You see how the elementary laws of formation appear, from simple to complex. The intrafigural stage gives you the elements, the interfigural stage is the beginning of seeing things in relation to one another, and algebraization is the discovery of structures. It can't be done any other way. If you began with structures and ended with a description of the elements, you'd be reversing an order that is, as I call it, "natural" because it's required, so to speak, by the very nature of things.

Bringuier: Each stage needs the preceding one?

Piaget: Yes, that's it. The stages are sequential.

Bringuier: I wonder; but that's probably because I don't understand very well. If ultimately every child covers the whole route for himself, without knowing it, why hasn't the history of science moved more rapidly?

Piaget: Because, once again, the child doesn't have a theory. You have to distinguish planes within knowledge—the plane of action and the plane of conceptualization. For the child, the actions are a function of a real problem, a problem set before him, and he doesn't think beyond that.

Bringuier: What about theorization?

Piaget: Theorization translates what is discovered by actions into concepts and doctrines.

Bringuier: One understands what one has found.

Piaget: Yes. In every field, action comes first, classification and conceptualization come later. Before science there were techniques, and, as Essertier has said, "The mechanic is a physicist unaware of physics and unaware of theory."

Bringuier: In short, in these analogies between human progress and individual development, one again finds the relationships that exist between action and theory in the taking of conscious-ness?

Piaget: Yes, exactly! It's one of the most striking parallels be-tween the two mechanisms. In every period of the history of mathematics—and physics, too, in part—the scholar, the inven-tor, the creator, uses instruments of which he is not conscious. Euclid constantly used "displacement groups," as they are now called, but the idea of "group" didn't appear until Galois. It's always present in Euclid, but in action, without the taking of consciousness. And the Greeks scorned algebra, considering it not to be a science, like geometry, but a trickery internal to the subject who used certain procedures to arrive at the discovery of geometric truths. Then, with Viète's algebra and Descartes's analytical geometry, I'd say we reach a historical phase of taking consciousness of operations—operations that Euclid used without arranging them by topic or incorporating them into a theory. Theory started with Galois . . . first with Descartes and Viète in the seventeenth century and, of course, Newton, geometry, and differential and integral calculus. But the Greeks had already used these operations. In this case, action had long preceded the taking of consciousness. Then, to give a recent example, the Bourbakis constructed a remarkable theory of mathematical structures by reducing them to three types of mother structures: algebraic structure, structures of order, and topological struc-tures. And do you know how they built up the structures? Not schematically—the schematic came afterwards. They built them by a series of comparisons—by a process Dieudonné called "inductive"—consisting of comparing various quite distinct mathematical topics in the effort to find the common structure. In the process they used a set of techniques about which they didn't theorize because it was their instrument for the discovery of structures. The theory came later; it's called the theory of morphisms and categories, developed later by Mac Lane and Eilenberg.

Bringuier: And you've worked on it too.

Piaget: Of course we used it for studying the child, to find the role of morphisms relative to the role of operations.

Bringuier: Morphisms? Will you define the term?

Piaget: It means "setting up correspondences."

Bringuier: It's a comparison.

Piaget: A comparison, yes. We make comparisons to find common forms in differing systems. A morphism is a correspondence that preserves the structure. We can say that one group is isomorphic to another group because it has the same structure. Direct operations, inverse operations, associativity . . .

Bringuier: Is the comparison made between terms?

Piaget: It could be anything: between terms, between relations, between transformations, between structures—it's the whole set of comparisons. But in studying operations, which we've been doing for years, what we had in mind was mostly the analysis of transformations. A comparison doesn't modify the terms it compares; if it did, there would be no comparison. But a transformation is the modification of a state in order to lead it to another state.

Bringuier: You carried out the study of morphisms with children?

Piaget: Yes. Our concern is still the similarities between the development of science, and of knowledge in general, and its formation in man. From the time a great many contemporary mathematicians took up morphisms and categories as a central issue, I wondered whether something might be found in the development of the child, and what role it played.

Bringuier: And did you find something?

Piaget: I did. Of course.

Bringuier: Isn't that because one always finds what one's looking for?

Piaget: We might have found nothing at all.

Bringuier: I thought the real world was bountiful enough to have an answer for every question.

Piaget: No, but we weren't asking, "Are there morphisms?" That's obvious, because it's the technique of every comparison. The question was, what is the relation between morphisms and transformations? Which is master? Is it the comparative aspect, or is it the creative and formative aspect of transformations, as I had always thought? And I found that, in the evolution of morphisms, they become increasingly subordinated to transformations. Clearly, transformations are master.

Bringuier: What do you mean by "transformations"?

Piaget: A transformation is an operation that transforms one state into another. For example, a negation, an inverse operation, in the displacement group is to go from *A* to *B* or to return from *B* to *A*. The return is the transformation of the direct operation.

Bringuier: Through reversibility.

Piaget: Yes. Or it could be composition, addition, anything.

Bringuier: You use the word "category." Is it like morphisms?

Piaget: Categories are systems of morphisms.

Bringuier: Particular ones.

Piaget: Particular ones. Particular and superior, having certain properties, such as "automorphism," as we say—the fact that one discovers the same system in the subsystems . . .

Bringuier: Within it.

Piaget: Yes, that's it.

Bringuier: A minute ago I said—and you didn't answer—"One always finds what one's looking for," and I added, "because the real world is bountiful enough to have an answer for every question." Since you obviously didn't like the way I put it, let me try to say it again: Don't you think the unknown is tamed? I mean, reality is summoned to appear when we question it and at no other time. We're willing to be surprised and discover it, but according to the standards we impose on it.

Piaget: I'm not so sure of that. The real world constantly invites us to ask new questions. The mistake . . .

Bringuier: But of the same type?

Piaget: Not necessarily. The problems in contemporary physics are still very new by comparison with Newton's physics. No, there is constant interchange between the questions we ask of reality and the unexpected answers that lead us to ask new questions.

Bringuier: Let's say that, for you, the questions and the answers are generally in the area of science.

Piaget: Agreed.

Bringuier: It's not possible for reality to teach us something about itself that falls outside the scientific mind?

Piaget: I don't think so.

Bringuier: That's because you're an Occidental.

Piaget: Why, yes.

Bringuier: You've been trained in Occidental science.

Piaget: If you like. But the Chinese have gone a very long way with their science.

Bringuier: Not as far as we have?

Piaget: It's entirely different; it began with dialectic instead of leading up to dialectic as a higher stage.

Bringuier: It began with dialectic? Would you explain?

Piaget: No, no. I'm not familiar enough with it. I got interested in Chinese science because of the book we're doing with Garcia. The problem was whether there is only one possible line of evolution in the development of knowledge or whether there may be different routes, which, of course, will lead to common points sooner or later. Well, Garcia, who is quite familiar with Chinese science, thinks they have traveled a route very different from our own. So I decided to see whether it is possible to imagine a psychogenesis different from our own, which would be that of the Chinese child during the greatest period of Chinese science, and I think that it is possible. Because in an act of knowledge, it's possible to focus on the object or to focus on the regulations that correct the different approaches leading to taking consciousness of the object; and in this case the dialectic would be more primitive than if you had focused on the object from the outset. But, please, I'm ahead of myself here; we're still writing the book, and it's premature to talk about a thing that still lacks adequate support, although I believe it without reservation.

> *Piaget's coauthor in the comparative study of individual development and scientific development is a physicist, Rolando Garcia; we asked him for his point of view.*[1]

Bringuier: As sketched out, the theory seems to imply that mankind, like the individual, passes from childhood to adulthood.

Garcia: No. Yes and no. If you go back to Aristotle, for example, it's clear that he created the logic that ruled science until the nineteenth century. But if you explore Aristotle's physics—and Piaget gave you some examples—you find explanations remarkably like the ones that children give.

Bringuier: Does it correspond to an adolescence or a childhood?

Garcia: The childhood of empirical science. But logical and mathematical science were developed before empirical science. And someone like Aristotle, who looms large in the history of thought, is just a child as far as physics is concerned. It's clear from Piagetian theory why the development of logic and mathematics preceded the development of physics and how and why Aristotle's thought is the way it is. That is, you can look at Aristotle's explanations of movement—movement of projectiles or falling weights—and see the same point of view that children have. But what's important for us isn't the subject matter but the mechanism of empirical thinking, the attribution to reality of certain logical laws; and here the child's point of view coincides with Aristotle's. It doesn't mean that Aristotle thought like a child! *(Silence.)* The mechanics are the same, not the subject matter. In modern mathematics, at the level of algebraic

1. Rolando Garcia was trained in theoretical physics; his work has been in fluid mechanics and dynamic meteorology.

geometry, of quantum mechanics, although it's at a much higher level of abstraction, you find the same mechanisms in action—the processes of the development of knowledge or the cognitive system are constructed according to the same kinds of evolutionary laws. This is what I consider Piaget's most significant contribution. I've done no more than pinpoint moments in the history of science that confirm what Piaget has shown about the child and the adolescent.

Bringuier: Don't you think that in both cases—the history of science and the formation of man's mind—there is too much determinism, too few crossroads, too little freedom? As you've described the system, or as Piaget has described it, it isn't clear why a certain idea should appear—in the history of science, for instance, why one type of inquiry appears rather than another.

Garcia: No, you have to make a distinction: a system can be determined but not be predictable; once one has a certain evolution, it's possible to explain why each stage is, so to speak, "determined" by the preceding one.

Bringuier: By going backward?

Garcia: But it doesn't mean that, having come to a certain point in the evolution of a system, one can predict the later evolution. There are relations to the preceding stages but no precise determination. There is an element of randomness that lets the system follow different schemas, which can't be predicted.

You know, for a long time we've not been able to speak of physics as a system that explains nature. Nature can be explained in bits and pieces, so to speak. There are time scales, spatial scales; some phenomena can be selected, and we can explain how, if one has a certain situation, there will be a certain consequence. But laws embracing all of nature, or predictions of what will happen at some moment in the future—we now know it's impossible. Nature is much more complicated than they imagined in Newton's time, when they formulated the great laws of nature.

Bringuier: But in light of what you've said, doesn't Jean Piaget's undertaking, which seems to be an attempt to embrace

"Everything one teaches a child one prevents him from inventing or discovering." (*Photo Christian Taillanier—L'Express*)

The theory of genetic epistemology was slowly born here, in this room forbidden to the household, in the midst of a jumbled battlefield of books, notes, and accumulated dossiers. No matter what direction you try to give to the conversation, Piaget always leads you back to his interest of the moment, to the present state of the work, the work in progress, the work that is under way. (*Photos Institut National de l'Audiovisuel*)

Never a hard and fast routine, never a vacation: work is a pleasure that never ends. He made his first observations on his own children; the garden is an annex of his office; he stops only on Saturdays for long bicycle rides to the nearby mountains. (*Photos Institut National de l'Audiovisuel*)

all of reality by means of the general field of knowledge—isn't it too inclusive, too all-encompassing?

Garcia: No, I don't think so. I'm very pleased with this formulation because it seems to me that Piaget is generally misunderstood. It's true that perhaps the ambition—I don't know if it's Piaget's ambition—but the intention of genetic epistemology is to give a general description and an inclusive explanation of knowledge. But giving an inclusive explanation of knowledge doesn't mean having a theory by means of which one can predict something about the future or dictate the laws of every development in the field of human knowledge; it simply means finding the unity there is in the human being as biological being, child, "common" man, and scientist and finding the unity of development, not through a unified, reductive theory, but through the discovery of the mechanisms common . . .

Bringuier: To those ensembles?

Garcia: to the biological being, the cognitive process, and the development of science. And it means that one can explain the development of knowledge itself by starting with biology; in other words, it is the developing biological being that becomes a thinking being, even a scientist, capable of making systems that explain nature—not *the* system that explains nature but some systems that explain parts of nature. And you see, the liberty you speak of is there, but between two poles: the individual himself—limited by his own capacities, his nervous system—and reality itself, which is stubborn, as someone at the symposium said; that is, it isn't easy to interpret.

Bringuier: Easy to construct?

Garcia: Construct, grasp, structure in any way. Reality can't be structured if it isn't structurable; that is to say, you can't structure it as you like—you can do it in one way but not in another. As Piaget has said, depending on whether the operations are good or bad, reality offers resistance or it doesn't.

Bringuier: How did you happen to get acquainted with M. Piaget?

Garcia: I knew Piaget's work when I was defending a completely different philosophical position. I was in logical empiricism as a student of Carnap at Chicago and of Reichenbach at Los Angeles.

Bringuier: You were a deserter.

Garcia: The first time I came in contact with Piaget's work, I completely rejected it as something almost banal. It was through my wife, a psychologist who had worked with Piaget's psychology, that I began to penetrate the problem and see that Piaget's explanations really went much further than any of the explanations offered by logical empiricism. Then I took stock of myself. I had the opportunity to come to Geneva. Piaget invited me to participate in the sessions at the Center for Epistemology, and for me it was like discovering a completely different world. You might say it completely changed my life—changed my way of thinking and my perspective on the world—and solved many of the questions I was asking.

> *Here is the testimony of another physicist, one who "reacted" in a slightly different but related and complementary way to the general problems of contemporary physics and to Piaget's structuralism. Ilia Prigogine is a specialist in the irreversible phenomena of thermodynamics. Like Rolando Garcia, he participated in the 1976 symposium, but it was his first time.*

Prigogine:[2] Today we realize how limited the schemas of clas-

2. Ilia Prigogine is one of the brightest representatives of the new physics. As theoretician of open systems in thermodynamics, he introduced the concept of *dissipative structures* to characterize those physical or chemicophysical phenomena that are unstable, fluctuating widely from the state of equilibrium. It is a vast and fundamental field, extending from gas molecules in reactors to that "macrosystem far from equilibrium," the human being.

The world that the scholar observes is dynamic and open. This is what, at the outset, brought Prigogine close to Jean Piaget.

sical physics are and how an increasing number of phenomena are reducible to games rather than to the notion of a classical law. I will tell you that my friend and colleague, Eigen, a distinguished German physicochemist, has just written a book that will certainly be translated into French soon; it's called *The Game*. For him, the basic thing is the game, with all that that implies in the way of freedom and choice. And we also have a practically new branch of mathematics, the theory of bifurcations, which shows that at a certain moment systems choose among possibilities—possibilities that a determinist theory, a macroscopic theory, even a Newtonian theory, doesn't allow to be taken into account.

Bringuier: You said "freedom." The term is generally applied to man.

Prigogine: Of course, human freedom is even higher—in fact, much higher in a hierarchy and much more complex. Nevertheless, it isn't so distant as all that, because it's probable that the mechanisms in the brain, the neurophysiological mechanisms, are also governed by nonlinear operations presenting this type of bifurcation. So that, in reality, the distance isn't perhaps as great as one might think at first glance. I believe this is an evolution coming into being, taking shape, and it's no accident if I, as a physicist, emphasize that particular aspect.

At the level of the study of structures, which is one of Jean Piaget's preoccupations, you have to understand that the problem of structure is relatively recent in physics, whereas it's classic in biology and anthropology. That's because in physics we've focused on the problem of equilibrium structure, with traditional physics seeking chiefly what is permanent. But more and more in physics we're also studying the coherent structures of nonequilibrium, in which an enormous number of molecules have a more *particular* spatiotemporal behavior—a behavior that is possible only because the system interacts with the world around it. You can see the relevance to Jean Piaget's theories. There is the identical paradox that, in order to have a structure in a really serious sense, the system under consideration must belong to a larger world.

Bringuier: A metasystem.

Prigogine: A metasystem. And there, obviously, we return to more immediate observations: this morning, at the symposium, I used the city as an example. It's clear that a city exists as a space-time structure only because it is included in the whole country. Also, if you look at a biological cell, you have catalysts, you have molecules transforming returning molecules; and the catalysts, the enzymes, are not distributed at random—they are themselves arranged in a certain order, a little bit like machine tools in a factory. That's a functional order, a structural order, an order in which function and structure are in correspondence. Now in a crystal, for example, you don't have function, though you certainly have a structure; but the whole is dead, it doesn't consume energy. That's why I've introduced the term "dissipative structure" for this kind of structure as opposed to the equilibrium structures of classical physics.

Bringuier: Now I see why you're a bit troubled by the term "equilibration" in Jean Piaget's vocabulary.[3]

Prigogine: Perhaps it's just a question of vocabulary: in order to speak of equilibration, it seems to me that there has to be an equilibrium conceived somehow in advance. Equilibration can't

3. This is an allusion to an exemplary discussion at the 1976 symposium (just published as *Epistémologie génétique et Equilibration: Colloque en l'honneur de Jean Piaget* [Neuchâtel and Paris: Delachaux & Niestlé]). It is exemplary in the sense that it clearly shows a misunderstanding that developed from the use of a word, and all its implications, exactly according to the schema Cellerier and Carreras suggested in 1969 (see chapter 7, part 2). The discussion is not simply a formal one, because it treats one of Piaget's essential ideas. Before introducing the idea of equilibration to the heat of symposium debate, the "boss" had written a book on the subject, *Equilibration des structures cognitives,* with the eloquent subtitle, *Problème central du développement.* It lies, in fact, at the heart of constructivism and open systems in Piaget's terms, along with the teleonomy of the subject, and so forth. It is a part of the theory he has ceaselessly continued to refine since writing the novel *Recherche,* in which it was first suggested.

be seen as working toward something that doesn't yet exist. You would be assuming a more or less static harmony, but we have no reason to think that any such preestablished harmony exists. That's why I prefer the word "innovation." Faced with a certain disequilibrium, often provoked by the activity of the subject, one has the impression that the subject tends toward a new cognitive schema. In this case, would you speak of equilibration or innovation?

Bringuier: The answer given was: stimulus, transformation provoked by the appearance of a new problem that had to be solved . . .

Prigogine: But are these perturbations? Or are they internal activities? Whether you take systems of molecules far from equilibrium, systems of neurons, cells in an organism, individuals in a society—if you want to think about mechanisms of innovation, the random element must be present. It seems to me that there's something a bit too causal, too deterministic, in the vocabulary that's being used.[4]

Bringuier: How did you meet Jean Piaget?

Prigogine: The first time I met Jean Piaget was at a conference in Copenhagen organized by a friend of mine, Leon Rosenfeld, who has since died. Leon Rosenfeld was a devoted follower of Niels Bohr, but he was also strongly attracted to Piaget. He often came to Geneva and often spoke to me about Piaget's work. Now, having known Bohr well and knowing a bit about Piaget, I can easily see what they have in common. Basically, it's the importance of the role of the man in the scientific theory he develops. In this respect, there is really something very different

4. In addition to the answers Piaget naturally gave to this criticism at the same symposium (see note 3, above), another reply to the argument was given by the physicist Rolando Garcia in the interview on pages 102–3, above.

from classical physics in Piaget and Bohr. Classical physics, what is often called "Galilean idealization," consists in believing that an independent entity really exists.

Bringuier: In itself?

Prigogine: In itself, and that we can attain to it.

Bringuier: As in Plato?

Prigogine: As in Plato, by a . . . maybe by a miracle, by the coincidence of our mathematics with the mathematics of the universe; in fact, the manner is pretty poorly defined. This was the point of view Einstein defended: a reality independent of man, absolute, that one could attain to with the aid of science. There is a famous discussion between Einstein and Tagore, the great Hindu poet and philosopher. Tagore asked Einstein, "If such a reality exists, how would it be accessible to us, how can we communicate with the absolute?" And, at bottom, the effort made by Bohr and Piaget is to make us understand how much we are attached to the description we give of the universe. How much we are implicated in it. You ask me, "Why don't we know how certain things are going to happen?"; but we are not God in our descriptions. We describe nature in a certain way, starting from the specific position we're in. Clearly, you can say to yourself, "God himself probably knows what's going to happen," but that is not our goal. We don't want to do physics as God would do it; we want to do physics by taking into account a certain type of information that's accessible to us as human beings; and then, having a certain biological constitution . . . [5] And this isn't

5. All are agreed on this central point. Piaget was the first, and he built the keystone to the system. I still remember his words at the conclusion of our 1969 conversations:

"For me, mathematics is in nature, and nature encompasses the human mind; the human mind develops it with the body, the nervous system. The whole surrounding organism itself belongs to physical nature, in such a way that there is harmony between mathematics and the real world through the organism, and not through physical experience bearing on objects . . . The human mind is a product of biological organization, a refined and superior product, granted, but still a product like any other."

subjectivism. On the contrary, it's a recognition of our position within the description we make.

Bringuier: It's realism itself?

Prigogine: It's realism itself. And then, basically, our description becomes a self-consistent thing. We describe the world, we describe the objects in this world, and we ourselves are objects in this world.

The Phenocopy

> Someday the phenomena of thought will appear as homologues of the phenomena of life.
> *Engels*

Bringuier: In fact, there's a single word for the whole of your work—a word I once heard you use; it's "constructivism."

Piaget: Yes, that's exactly right. Knowledge is neither a copy of the object nor taking consciousness of a priori forms predetermined in the subject; it's a perpetual construction made by exchanges between the organism and the environment, from the biological point of view, and between thought and its object, from the cognitive point of view.

Bringuier: You've just used the word "biology." Have you come back to biology?

Piaget: Well, I haven't come back to it—I've never left it.

Bringuier: I know it relates to the studies . . .

Piaget: Oh, yes, but I've found new facts. *(Silence. He thinks about the best way to present this.)* The major problem in knowledge, since it isn't a copy of reality, a copy of objects, is the way it reconstructs reality. In other words, reality must be known, of course, but by recreating it through deduction and endogenous construction. So, in biology, the main problem is the relation between the organism and the environment, a relation that was simple for Lamarck, because he believed in the inheritance of acquired characteristics, those that arose as a function of the environment.

Bringuier: That's been dropped.

Piaget: Well, when nothing was found to confirm the theory of the inheritance of acquired characteristics, the neo-Darwinists used random variation, chance mutation, and so forth, to explain everything, with selection afterwards, as if this subsequent selection were a sufficient explanation for the precision with which animals' organs fit the environment.

Bringuier: And it doesn't satisfy you.

Piaget: No. First, the psychological equivalent seems inconceivable to me. It amounts to saying that every instance of knowledge has an aleatory point of departure and that our understanding comes from a series of random moves, of which we retain the successful ones and eliminate the rest. It removes all idea of the necessity intrinsic to knowledge. So in terms of human knowledge and theory of knowledge, which is my main concern, but even in terms of animal knowledge—that is, behavior—I find the explanation very unsatisfactory.

Bringuier: So?

Piaget: In certain cases there has been adduced as evidence what Waddington called "genetic assimilation" and others call "phenocopy": the replacement of a variation that begins by being nonhereditary—phenotypical, as they say—replacement of this by a genotypical variation, a hereditary variation.

Bringuier: Don't tell me you've started to work on the lymnaea again, after fifty years!

Piaget: My interest in the lymnaea was renewed because, on opening Waddington's new book, *L'Evolution d'un évolutionniste*—he was kind enough to send me one shortly before he died—I happened to find a whole chapter on my lymnaea.

Waddington cited this record as the most positive case of "genetic assimilation," as he calls it, in nature. It's often been seen in the laboratory, but this is a case from nature. Roughly, you see, the species is elongated in stagnant water and contracted in turbulent water. As the waves beat against it, the animal presses itself against the rocks, thus increasing the size of the opening, as it increases during growth. In doing this, the snail pulls on the muscle attached to the whorl, which shortens it in comparison to the whorls of marshland forms. The lacustrine forms, as they are called, may be phenotypical only: if you put them in an aquarium, their descendants are elongated, as in the marsh forms, but others, in the turbulent water of the great lakes—Léman, Neuchâtel, and Boden—are fixed. If you raise these in an aquarium, they continue to occur in the contracted form, and if you put them in a pond, as I did on the Vaudois Plateau, they still keep the contracted form. So here is a typical case of a phenotypical form, appearing only in very specific environments, like the rough water of a major lake, being replaced by a genotype of the same form. But primarily I've studied the sedums ...

Bringuier: the garden plants ...

Piaget: looking for cases of phenocopy, as I've just defined it. To take a simple example: a common species of sedum occurs in a very small form, a dwarf form, when it grows at an altitude of 1,900 to 2,000 meters. But the dwarf form is not hereditary; when you bring the plant back down to the plains, it returns to its normal height. On two or three peaks, however, the small variety appears to be fixed and stable, and when it is brought back down to the plains—I've raised them here for years—it retains its high-altitude formation. Completely.

Bringuier: But doesn't this challenge traditional biology? It's the inheritance of acquired characteristics.

Piaget: Now, wait! That depends on how it's explained. If you explain it as a direct action of the environment of the genome ...

Bringuier: It's neo-Lamarckism!

Piaget: Of course it's Lamarckism, that's the long and short of it. But if you explain it as Waddington does, with "genetic as-similation," or the way I'm going to try to, with the concept of phenocopy, it's a reconstruction by selection, but a selection imposed, as I see it, by the internal environment. The high-altitude phenotype . . .

Bringuier: Let's define phenotype again.

Piaget: The phenotype is the nonhereditary variation. It's the variation that occurs in a certain environment and may change with a change of environment. So the phenotype does not act directly on the genome—far from it; it acts on the internal environment. During growth, you see, the internal environment and the so-called epigenetic environment—everything that . . . the successive stages of growth . . .

Bringuier: The cellular environment.

Piaget: Yes, but not cellular only; the whole organism is modified by the phenotype. Then, if there has been disequilibrium, if the internal environment is too disturbed, and if, in the end, the regulatory genes are affected, new variations are produced, genetic ones, produced by the genome.

Bringuier: Because the gene itself is transformed?

Piaget: No. Simply because it is informed that something isn't working right. This does not come as a message, as Lamarck thought; the genome is not informed of what is occurring in the soma and is certainly not informed of what is occurring in the external environment. But a disequilibrium, if one occurs, can little by little produce new variations. These variations will then be selected by the internal environment which has been modified by the phenotype. It's still selection, but not in the crude sense of survival in the external environment. It's a harmony with an internal environment that has become the new setting and to which hereditary variations must adapt by internal selection.

Bringuier: But this "harmony," then, is a kind of biological progress. It's almost finalism.

Piaget: Yes, of course, there's purpose, in Monod's teleonomic sense, in the sense that the whole epigenetic system is conditioned by a program. Of course the program is teleonomic; but the interesting thing about it is the endogenous reconstruction in a setting imposed by the phenotypical variation. It's not a direct action of the environment on the genome.

Bringuier: It's a reconsideration by . . .

Piaget: A reconstruction. And then you see right away a perfect parallel with what I maintain in regard to cognitive development; every piece of knowledge, every step of progress in our intelligence, every transformation of intelligence, is always an endogenous reconstruction of exogenous givens furnished by experience.

Bringuier: I'm always impressed by your permanent need for coherence, for linking things together as you go along, in a way that seems . . .

Piaget: Since I had a career first as a biologist and then as an epistemologist, there's no reason not to be coherent. They aren't all that different. They raise the same questions. Intelligence is an adaptation to the external environment just like every other biological adaptation.

Bringuier: Does this coherence give way to disorder? That's what they say these days in cybernetics, in information-processing: disorder is spoken of as productive terrain; in a lighter vein, in marketing, they do "brainstorming." Does your way of thinking allow for complete disorder, wandering thought? Do you see what I mean?

Piaget: Yes, more or less. But I wouldn't use the word "disorder" but rather "lacuna" and "possible contradiction." If the two systems were completely dissimilar, with biological development, on the one hand, and cognitive development, on the other, then I would feel that they presented an insurmountable disorder. I avoid just this kind of incoherence by always looking for links between related or different disciplines.

Bringuier: And this never ends?

Piaget: Obviously not.

Bringuier: You mentioned something to me once: the learning period of a kitten. The kitten progresses faster than a baby at first, then it stops; so it was of no benefit to the kitten to go more quickly.

Piaget: Yes.

Bringuier: And we ourselves spend a very long time learning about life and gaining knowledge. Does this go on all our lives? Are we open systems permanently, until we die?

Piaget: That's the ideal I personally strive for, to remain a child to the end. Childhood is the creative phase par excellence!

Bringuier: They say—this is a related idea—that man is born more "imperfect" than the monkey, for example. There, too, it's probably what lets him go further. Does man have a constructive breach?

Piaget: Please explain, I don't understand.

Bringuier: A gap—that is, something that lets him continuously reequilibrate himself, as you say.

Piaget: Ah, yes. Of course he does.

Bringuier: Something in him that is permanently open.

Piaget: Any new fact you find in one field, naturally, you're going to wonder if it has repercussions in related fields. If that's what you mean by the "gap," what I've called a "lacuna," certainly we work that way.

Bringuier: Then, too, don't the sciences always proceed in this fashion? By integrating phenomena that are marginal, little known, or random?

Piaget: Of course; it's just when you have the courage to see that something doesn't work that you find new things.

Bringuier: For this, do we have to have someone else tell us "You're mistaken," or is it within ourselves?

Piaget: Not always. Usually it's useful to have someone criticize you; but if a person is honest, he can do it by himself.

Bringuier: In your case, is criticism helpful? I have the impression it isn't very. Am I right?

Piaget: I'm considered to be the most systematic of thinkers . . .

one who has always, when proposing something, taken care not to be proved wrong later on.

Bringuier: What do you think of that opinion?

Piaget: It's accurate.

Bringuier: So you get no benefit from . . .

Piaget: Of course I see possible and latent contradictions, but I keep them to myself.

Bringuier: You store them up for later.

Piaget: Oh, I use them. *(Laughter.)*

Bringuier: I keep thinking about your way of returning unperturbed to ground you or others have already studied before.

Piaget: Of always going around in the same circle?

Bringuier: Yes, but not just that . . . of coming back on different levels to the same interests. To behavior, for example. It's a word or an idea you've had from the beginning. Cellerier says, "In all this theory, it's really behavior that sets the pace."

Piaget: Very recently I wrote a little book presenting an argument I deeply believe in, although it will seem bizarre to the majority of biologists: the prime mover of evolution is behavior.[1]

Bringuier: Rather than what?

Piaget: Rather than physicochemical transformations at the level of biochemistry. As Monod has quite accurately put it, the organism's basic characteristic, physiologically, is conservation, and variation is only a twist, what you might call a failure of the conservation mechanism. Well, this seems to me quite true for the basic physiology of the organism; there's no reason for it to vary if it's adapted. But behavior is constantly aiming to improve itself. The two objectives of behavior, when we speak of objectives, because every behavior pursues an end . . .

Bringuier: The desire to live . . .

Piaget: The two objectives of behavior are, first, the extension of the environment, having an environment larger than the pres-

1. *Le comportement, moteur de l'évolution* (Paris: Gallimard, Collection Idées, 1976).

ent one, for all sorts of reasons, if only as a precaution . . . to be able to see farther, if there are possible enemies . . .

Bringuier: To have something in reserve.

Piaget: To have something in reserve, and so forth. It's first the extension of the environment and, second, the increase, the growth, of the organism's powers over the environment. A growth that goes . . .

Bringuier: Predation.

Piaget: Yes, predation, locomotion, whatever you like. One of the most striking arguments is found in plant behavior. Some flowers turn toward the sun, and so forth. But plants do not have locomotion and don't act on the environment, as animals do, to displace objects. In other words, their behavior is extremely limited. Well, it seems to me that, compared to animal evolution, plant evolution is considerably less. There are fewer differences between a moss and an orchid than there are between an earthworm and a chimpanzee.

Bringuier: So the wealth of possible behavior has increased the rate of evolution?

Piaget: Possible and practiced! Yes, that's right.

Memory: The Kidnapping of Jean Piaget

Bringuier: Apart from your work at the Center, have you conducted other research?

Piaget: Yes, I have continued my research in collaboration with Barbel Inhelder; our latest study concerns the relation between memory and intelligence.[1] The problem is to learn whether memory consists essentially in the more or less passive reproduction of what has been perceived earlier, or whether it is a reconstitution—partly conceptual and partly inferential—of a past of which a part has been forgotten and has to be completed and reconstituted.

Bringuier: Isn't this about the same as what you were saying about reflection and the taking of consciousness?

Piaget: Yes, of course. It's an analogous problem, but bearing

---

1. B. Inhelder, Piaget's student and now a collaborator, has participated in one whole part of the theoretical elaboration. She is particularly interested in problems of strategy and functioning; in studying the logic of the child and the adolescent, problems of *apprentissage* (with H. Sinclair), she has developed and elaborated new forms of clinical experimentation and has invented a set of technical devices.

on memory, often thought of as the faithful image of a past that is simply copied by memory—its current representation.

Bringuier: That's not what it is.

Piaget: That's not it at all. What we've found in studying the stages of memory in operatory problems is that the child remembers what he's been shown as he understands it and not as he's seen or perceived or lived it. Here's a nice example from seriation: the child is given a group of sticks already arranged according to length, that is, arranged from the shortest to the longest in a regular stepwise progression, and he's told simply, "Look at this, then we'll wait a bit. Take a good look, then we'll put it away and you'll draw it without seeing anything, simply by remembering what I've shown you." He looks at the serial configuration for a minute and then, ten minutes later, we have him draw the picture. It might be an hour later. Now, what we've dicovered is that the child's drawings, what he thinks he saw in the material presented, correspond exactly to the way he himself constructs a seriation. In other words, at the first stage there isn't a series at all; the child draws pairs—a short and a long, a short and a long—but the groups are not coordinated. The result is something completely irregular but in pairs. Next come groups of three—a short, a medium, and a long, a short, a medium, and a long—but the groups of three are not coordinated. Next come short, incomplete series; instead of having ten sticks, there'll be only five, properly arranged; but he doesn't remember the rest. Finally, there is the complete seriation. All this corresponds exactly to the stage at which the child is in his construction of the series—not to his perception of the series. In these cases, memory is the memory of what he could have done or should have done to reproduce the proposed model.

Bringuier: That is, he's faithful to his present and not to his past?

Piaget: Right you are! He reconstitutes the past as a function of the present. What comes next is fascinating: three months or six months later—without, of course, having seen anything in the meantime—he is asked, "Do you remember what I showed you?" and he says, "Yes, of course, they were little sticks," and so forth. "Draw me a picture of what I showed you." Well, after three or six months, his memory is considerably better than after ten minutes or an hour. In other words, "memory" now is the memory or the image of the scheme and not of the object—the action scheme that let him construct the object; and since the scheme has progressed in six months, the child reconstitutes an object he has been shown but could reproduce only poorly at the time he saw it. Of all the children studied, 75 percent showed some progress over their immediate memory of it. We've seen this happen not only with seriation but with many other operatory schemes.

Bringuier: How old are the children?

Piaget: Between five and eight. By the time they're eight, they show the whole series after a brief time.

Bringuier: Does this cast light on other sorts of memory? Affective memory, for instance?

Piaget: Certainly. You asked me before for my reservations about Freudianism. I have the greatest mistrust of childhood memories used by psychoanalysts, because I believe they are largely reconstituted, and I'll give you a proof of what I'm saying . . .

> *(It should be mentioned here that Jean Piaget spent part of his childhood in Paris with his French-born grandmother; they lived on the Avenue d'Antin, which has since been renamed Franklin Roosevelt Avenue. He continues:)*

Piaget: Well, I have a childhood memory of my own that would be absolutely spendid if it were authentic, because it goes back to an age when one doesn't usually have memories of childhood. I was still in a baby carriage, taken out by a nurse, and she took me down the Champs-Elysées, near the Rond-

Point. I was the object of an attempted kidnapping. Someone
tried to grab me out of the buggy. The straps held me in, and the
nurse scuffled with the man, who scratched her forehead; something worse might have happened if a policeman hadn't come by
just then. I can see him now as if it were yesterday—that was
when they wore the little cape that comes down to here *(he mo-
tions with his hand)* and carried a little white stick, and all that,
and the man fled. That's the story. As a child I had the glorious
memory of having been the object of an attempted kidnapping.
Then—I must have been about fifteen—my parents received a
letter from the nurse, saying that she had just been converted and
wanted to confess all her sins, and that she had invented the
kidnapping story herself, that she had scratched her own
forehead, and that she now offered to return the watch she'd
been given in recognition of her courage. In other words, there
wasn't an iota of truth in the memory. And I have a very vivid
memory of the experience, even today. I can tell you just where it
happened on Champs-Elysées, and I can still see the whole thing.

Bringuier: But in fact it was just a family story?

Piaget: I must have heard it when I was, oh, I don't know, seven
or eight. My mother must have told someone that an attempt
had been made to kidnap me. I heard the story and probably
even heard her whispering—you don't tell a child that he was
practically kidnapped, for fear of upsetting him—but at any rate,
I overheard the story, and, starting from that, I reconstituted the
image—such a beautiful image that even today it seems a memory of something I experienced.

Bringuier: It's engraved in your memory?

Piaget: Yes. Now, suppose the memory had been accurate,
that everything happened just as the nurse told it. It still wouldn't
be a direct memory, but a reconstituted memory—reconstituted
by means of the story I heard later. So I'm fairly skeptical
of childhood memories. I know that the way a child reconstitutes his own memories, or an adult reconstitutes his childhood memories, can be useful psychoanalytically. But ultimately,

I don't think they are pure memories; I don't believe in pure memories; they always presuppose a greater or lesser degree of inference.

Bringuier: But if I were a psychoanalyst, I would probably say that the psychoanalytic experience—beyond such distortions created at subsequent moments of life—consists precisely of re-membering, reliving, the event itself, what really happened, through the phenomenon of transference, and so forth. There, that's an answer to your criticism.

Piaget: No, what that operation gives you is the individual's present notion of his past, not his direct knowledge of that past. And I believe that it's Erikson—a nonorthodox psychoanalyst, but one with whom I fully agree—who says that the past is re-constructed as a function of the present just as much as the present is explained by the past. There is interaction. Whereas, for the orthodox Freudian, the past determines the adult's present behavior. So how do you know the past? You know it through memories that are themselves reconstituted in a context, and it is the context of the present and as a function of the present.

Bringuier: And through the epic of memories of memories.

Piaget: Right. So I'm not saying it isn't important; but it's much more complex than simply the utilization of childhood memories.

Bringuier: In fact, one could say that if you have a criticism of Freudianism, it would be not so much that it makes fundamental and glaring errors as that it lacks subtlety.

Piaget: Yes, that's so. I think there is a basic truth in Freudian-ism; but everything must still be developed and reexamined in the light of contemporary psychology.

Bringuier: Hasn't analysis ever tempted you?

Piaget: But I was analyzed!

Bringuier: You were analyzed?

Piaget: Please, one has to know what one's talking about when one speaks of something.

Bringuier: You were . . .

Piaget: I had a didactic analysis with one of Freud's students. Every morning at eight o'clock for eight months.

Bringuier: Here?

Piaget: In Geneva. She was one of Freud's students from eastern Europe and had been analyzed by him. Yes, of course, I've been analyzed—if not, I wouldn't be talking about analysis!

Bringuier: Why did you stop?

Piaget: I stopped because I was . . . Everything I saw in it was interesting. It was marvelous to discover all one's complexes. But my psychoanalyst learned that I was impervious to the theory and that she'd never convince me. She told me it wasn't worthwhile to continue.

Bringuier: Essentially, you were resisting it, then?

Piaget: Yes, but theoretially, not at all in the application of the analysis. She'd been sent to Geneva by the Société Internationale de Psychanalyse to disseminate the doctrine. It was around 1921. I was perfectly willing to be a guinea pig. As I said, I found it very interesting, but the doctrine was something else again. In the interesting facts that psychoanalysis showed, I didn't see the need for the interpretation she tried to impose on them. She's the one who stopped.

Bringuier: But how could that have bothered her in your analysis?

Piaget: You see, it wasn't a therapeutic situation or even a didactic psychoanalysis, since I didn't intend to become a psychoanalyst; it was propaganda in the best sense of the term, an extension of the doctrine; she felt it wasn't worth wasting an hour a day on a man who wouldn't accept the theory.

Bringuier: You would have like to go on, then?

Piaget: Oh, yes, I was very interested. For instance, I'm not the least bit visual. I couldn't tell you what color the wall-hangings in this study are without looking at them. Well, it was simply remarkable how many visual images came back with childhood memories.

Bringuier: Ah, yes. And colors?

Piaget: Colors, everything. I was visual during the analytic hours in a way that really surprised me. I visualized scenes from the past, partly reconstituted, as I told you, but with a whole context, including shape and color—a precision I would have been incapable of at any other time.

Bringuier: Do you have any idea why you have eliminated visual things?

Piaget: My mind is abstract.

Bringuier: Is that why? So as not to be burdened . .

Bringuier: I don't know.

Piaget: by objects?

Bringuier: I don't know. No, I'm aural and motor. I can remember a tune perfectly for years—but visual, not at all.

Piaget: Do you like music?

Bringuier: Very much! It's surprising how music stimulates the brain.

Bringuier: Do you listen to music while you're working out problems?

Piaget: Yes.

Bringuier: Just any music?

Piaget: Oh, no, not at all.

Bringuier: What, then?

Piaget: Either highly structured music whose structure excites the mind—anything of Bach's, for example; or else dramatic passages—the Commendatore's arrival in *Don Giovanni,* or Wotan's Farewell in *Die Götterdämmerung,*[2] or Boris's death in *Boris Godunov.*

Bringuier: What is the appeal—the simple sentiments expressed or the music itself?

Piaget: The music itself!

Bringuier: Because there's a lot of difference between Wagner and Bach.

2. [Wotan's Farewell actually occurs in *Die Walküre,* not in *Die Götter-dämmerung.* Wotan in fact makes no appearance at all in the latter opera. —Trans.]

Piaget: Yes, but you see I use them—if I may put it crudely—in very different situations. The dramatic scenes are for general stimulation—for times when one is "dry" for quasi-emotional reasons, when one has no energy.

Bringuier: To start up the motor?

Piaget: To start up the motor. But Bach is for construction. Bach is for the brain, Wagner for the guts.

Bringuier: And Mozart?

Piaget: Oh, both. For both!

Bringuier: But in these cases you don't listen to the music. You hear it, but you don't listen to it.

Piaget: Well, it's a problem, but I think one manages nevertheless.

Bringuier: It's in the back of one's mind . . .

Piaget: No. No, there's a kind of synthesis. It still creates a unity.

Concerning Creativity: The Three Methods

(He lights his pipe again. I watch him.)

Bringuier: Is there any difference between scientific creativity such as yours and other types of creativity—a painter's or a writer's? Are they comparable?

Piaget: I have a hard time answering that because I'm not familiar with the other sorts of creativity.

Bringuier: Have you ever wondered about it?

Piaget: No, no. Never. A few years ago, some students at Johns Hopkins University in Baltimore organized a series of lectures on creativity and invited me to be one of their speakers. I talked about creativity in the child, of course. But they wanted to know how I got my own ideas. I was at quite a loss to answer them because I'd never really considered the question; but on thinking it over, I told them I had three methods.

Bringuier: Three?

Piaget: (He laughs.) Three! First: when you are working on something, read nothing in the field; read afterwards only. Second method: read as much as possible in related fields; for the study of intelligence, that would of course be biology on the one side; then there would be mathematics and logic and so on, including sociology—everything, in fact, related to one's subject. Third method: have a whipping boy. My whipping boy is logical positivism. I was pleased to see the American students applaud this, for it proves that that school of thought is on the decline. Logical positivism is a radical empiricism that holds that all knowledge comes from perception and, moreover, from language in the domain of logic and mathematics.

Bringuier: The whipping boy is used as a motive, it's used to advance . . . ?

Piaget: Yes, of course.

Bringuier: I'd still like to hear you elaborate on the first two points: read nothing in your own field, but read in related fields.

Piaget: It goes without saying that you should read nothing in your own field. If you approach a topic by reading everything that's been written on it, it's much harder to find new things; but if you move right ahead and make comparisons afterwards, you'll discover that you're either repeating what's already been done or that there are certain differences. These may be fruitful.

Bringuier: Then, too, I imagine that when you read what is written by people in your own intellectual field, you don't read, you take.

Piaget: (Laughter.) That's a polite way of saying "assimilate." Yes.

Bringuier: But you yourself don't take, you reject!

Piaget: That's right.

Bringuier: You recognize your own routes and areas in the routes and areas of others—and that's what you're interested in.

Piaget: If you like, yes.

Bringuier: The other scientist's way of thinking as such is really not very important to you.

Piaget: Yes, it is. Oh, yes, the . . .

Bringuier: Not his approach.

Piaget: On the contrary, if there's a difference of opinion, it's very fruitful. Of course. If you want to know who is right, you have to see, mainly, whether you can propose a better solution.

Bringuier: And why do you recommend reading in related fields?

Piaget: Related fields? Because I think any exploration of knowledge must by nature be interdisciplinary. It's impossible to dissociate real steps forward of the intelligence from logicians' and mathematicians' axiomatization or formalization of them, and so forth. It's impossible to isolate the individual from the social environment, and so forth.

Bringuier: But universities draw definite lines in teaching; there are sociology, biology, this, that. Nice labels.

Piaget: The question is whether that's a good thing or a catastrophe.

Bringuier: It's a catastrophe?

Piaget: Of course.

Bringuier: We've come back to what you said one day, the idea that whenever you teach a child something, you prevent him from inventing it. It's just what you're saying now. Because "to invent" is to move freely among disciplines.

Piaget: Yes, of course.

Bringuier: So if we take it a step further and make it political, in the broadest sense of the term, we might ask what system allows, or could allow, education to be just that? What kind of government, state, or society can do this best?

Piaget: You're asking questions that I'm not qualified to answer.

Bringuier: Yes and no. You're too modest. For example, I'm thinking of one year, I think it was about '52, in Melun, when, with Lichnerowicz and a few others—Dieudonné, I think—

Piaget: Dieudonné, yes.

Bringuier: You formulated principles for restructuring the teaching of mathematics.

Piaget: No, no.

Bringuier: What was that meeting about?

Piaget: No, no. That meeting had to do with comparing mental structures and mathematical structures.

Bringuier: And it didn't result in a teaching method?

Piaget: No.

Bringuier: Oh, I thought it did. Because it came afterwards, didn't it? Maybe not directly, but all teaching of mathematics has—fortunately—been affected, and the changes came from those years, didn't they?

Piaget: Yes, if you like.

Bringuier: And probably from that meeting?

Piaget: In part. I was able to show that the structures the child constructs spontaneously are much closer to modern—or so-called modern—mathematics than what was traditionally taught; so, of course, psychology can lend support to teachers of modern mathematics. But be careful! Modern mathematics must be taught by equally modern methods, not by old methods. Now the great mistake . . .

Bringuier: If not, it's a patchwork.

Piaget: Well, of course. So the great mistake some people have made is going to formalization too quickly with students who aren't at all ready to assimilate it. Modern mathematics should start with the child's mind and with what he already has in the way of roots for topology, group theory—for operations of structures generally. But if one hurries over this and tries to teach modern mathematics by the methods of modern mathematics, that is, formalization and axiomatic methods, everything is lost.

Bringuier: And, once again, they're imposing . . .

Piaget: Yes, they're imposing. Of course.

Bringuier: You said "What one finds already in the child, the roots." Where do these roots begin, what is the minimum given?

Piaget: Well, it begins even before language. I think the most creative period of human life is between birth and eighteen months. It's extraordinary how . . .

Bringuier: From the first reflex . . .

Piaget: Yes. To the construction of space, causality, time, the permanent object, and so on.

Bringuier: You learn more at that time than in all that remains?

Piaget: For speed and productivity, I've always found it to be the period of greatest creation. Cognitive creation. And don't forget—even before language—in action! Then, at the level of thought and representation, all this will be reconstructed, restructured, on conceptual ground, on the conceptual plane.

Bringuier: Can these stages be accelerated?

Piaget: There's no advantage to it.

Bringuier: Why not?

Piaget: Because everyone has his own rhythm, and it isn't easy to know what it is. The optimum rhythm has never been the subject of careful research.

Bringuier: The speed.

Piaget: The speed, yes. We mentioned the kitten advancing more quickly to the discovery of the permanent object than the baby does. It manages to do at four months what the baby can do only at nine or ten months, but then it stops. So it's not for nothing that the baby takes longer: he has more assimilations to make, and deeper ones. Going too quickly lessens the fruitfulness of later assimilation.

(Silence. He is thinking.)

Perhaps there is a common rhythm, an optimum speed, but I don't know. Everyone has his own. When you write a book, if you do it too quickly, it isn't good; if you do it too slowly, it isn't good either. There is an optimum rhythm in writing, just as in the creation of ideas.

Bringuier: Still, here and there—in America, probably—people dream of acceleration.

Piaget: Always.

Bringuier: Why?

(He shrugs his shoulders slightly and doesn't answer.)

Bringuier: Let me say this: you show reticence whenever I suggest consequences or applications of the theory. A few minutes ago I felt it with regard to the Melun meeting, and again just now. Pedagogical problems . . .

Piaget: Look! I have no opinion on pedagogy. I'm very interested in the problem of education, for I have the impression that an enormous amount needs to be reformed and transformed; but I think that the role of the psychologist is, above all, to give the facts the pedagogue can use and not to put oneself in his place and give him advice. It's the pedagogue's job to see how he can use what we offer. Pedagogy is not simply applied pedagogy; it's a whole set of techniques the specialist has to fit together by himself.

Bringuier: Still, do you have the feeling that your theoretical works have influenced pedagogy? We talked about mathematics in this connection.

Piaget: Yes, some of them.

Bringuier: Not generally?

Piaget: No. As for modern mathematics taught to children, in that case there is an astonishing convergence with what we have learned in psychology. And in that case there may be direct application. But we've just mentioned the difficulties! Besides—and it's remarkable—absolutely nothing is done to teach the child the spirit of experimentation. He has lessons, he sees experiments demonstrated; but seeing them is not the same as doing them for himself. I'm convinced that one could develop a marvelous method of participatory education by giving the child the apparatus with which to do experiments and thus discover a lot of things by himself. Guided, of course. But in fact it would have to be a professional who could see how this would work in practice.

Bringuier: I see—and I'm not taking up pedagogy!—you're

suggesting a certain concept of education that isn't usually encountered.

Piaget: No, it isn't. Education, for most people, means trying to lead the child to resemble the typical adult of his society.

Bringuier: To be like the men it needs.

Piaget: That's right. But for me, education means making creators, even if there aren't many of them, even if the creations of one are limited by comparison with those of another. But you have to make inventors, innovators, not conformists.

Bringuier: Do you think that every individual can be a creator?

Piaget: In varying degrees, of course; there is always a field in which he can be one.

Bringuier: You're talking about creativity. A minute ago, you suggested some tricks of your own. Three tricks.

Piaget: Not tricks. Methods.

Bringuier: Methods, then. But talent isn't a question of method, it's something else. What is talent?

(Silence. Very long.)

Piaget: That's the secret. The most mysterious secret.

Bringuier: That's a funny answer for a scientist to give.

Piaget: No, it's the least well-known problem in the psychology of intelligence. Every scientist who has tried to identify the factors and conditions of genius has run into a stone wall; because it just isn't very clear. It's not a funny answer. It's admitting a gap.

Bringuier: But someday we'll know?

Piaget: I hope so. Why not?

Bringuier: Is it a problem you care about personally?

Piaget: Oh, of course. One of my former collaborators, a colleague in the United States, Gruber, spends all his time at present studying the genesis of ideas in scientists and geniuses, using Darwin. It's unbelievable how complex the problem is. Darwin beat around the bush three or four years to discover something that was logically implied by what he had said four years earlier. It's a hell of a problem.

The Students, the University. Basic and Applied Research

Bringuier: How are your relationships with the students?

Piaget: They're usually excellent, but, since the student uprisings, you never know what will happen.

Bringuier: Since May 1968?

Piaget: Since May. In terms of exams, for instance. The ones in July went well. Afterwards, each student was polled for his impression of each professor; my exams were judged to be . . . well, not standard, but intelligent. The students weren't protesting, you know.

Bringuier: What do you think the ideal university would be?

Piaget: Oh, there'd be research at every level, and seminars based on the research.

Bringuier: With a minimum of course work?

Piaget: Yes.

Bringuier: When you teach classes, then, you're acting against your own ideas?

Piaget: Well, I usually stop after twenty minutes and ask for questions or objections. That way, it works. Sometimes it falls flat; other times there's lively resistance from the class, and it's a pleasure.

Bringuier: You're both a theoretician and a practitioner

because you do experiments. What do you think, generally, of the relationship between basic research and applied research?

Piaget: I think basic reserach is too often forgotten.

Bringuier: You mean, not enough money is allocated for it?

Piaget: Among other things. No, basic research has considerable importance; but specialists in applied research are tempted not to improve on basic research at the very point where their applications would have some bearing.

Bringuier: Basic research presupposes the long term, whereas the people with decision-making powers, those who hold the purse strings, are dedicated to the short term?

Piaget: That's right. Chiefly, basic research leads to practical applications that are absolutely unforeseen; whereas, if you are looking for an application, are devoted to applied research, you restrict the problems and choose the ones that, ultimately, are the least productive for the application itself. Maxwell, with his symmetric equations, did ten times more for technical application than the men of his time who worked only in applied research. All of Maxwell's equations in electrodynamics, you recall, done for elegance and the need to complete a system, to generalize it, and so forth—all that was the work of a pure mathematician guided by a concern for symmetry that led to a remarkable theory, in terms of doctrine. But as technical application, it's the whole of electricity and the whole of technique— radio and whatever else you can name! All that sprang from Maxwell's equations!

Bringuier: You spent some time at Princeton. Did you meet Einstein?

Piaget: Oh, yes, and we also corresponded. What was extraordinary about him was his youthfulness of mind, his ability to be interested in practically everything, his wanting to hear about almost anything—child psychology, for instance.

Bringuier: Did he find it entertaining?

Piaget: At first. But when he understood the problems—which happened at once—he immediately saw the whole. He'd say, "This is what you're looking for."

Bringuier: The speed . . .

Piaget: Absolutely incredible! He could see instantly what lay behind.

Bringuier: What did he find especially interesting in your work?

Piaget: There was the problem of speed and time—he had recommended it to me earlier; we wanted to see if there was a primitive intuition of speed. But what attracted him most, when I saw him at Princeton again, were problems of conservation.

Bringuier: What would that be? Modeling clay?

Piaget: The transfer of liquids especially. You pour water into a glass of a certain shape, then into a glass of another shape, without changing the quantity. It was a delight to him to see what detours and complications you have to go through for the simplest bit of knowledge. He'd say, "It's more complicated than physics!"

Bringuier: Oppenheimer?

Piaget: I knew him too, but we had less time—he was busy.

Bringuier: When did you meet him?

Piaget: At the same time, '53—'53 to '54—at the Princeton Institute, of which Einstein was a member.

Bringuier: Oppenheimer must have been deeply affected by the atom-bomb affair?

Piaget: Yes, he had an underlying sadness after his troubles.

Bringuier: Do you think they were right to make it? The bomb?

Piaget: Of course not! No. And Oppenheimer was convinced of that.

Bringuier: They made it because they were afraid the German physicists would.

Piaget: Yes, of course. So how could they have done otherwise? They would have made it anyway.

Bringuier: You?

Piaget: Nazism presented such a danger . . .

New Possibilities (June 1976)

> How can one attain to something new?
> Perhaps that is my central problem.
> *Jean Piaget*

Piaget: Right now what we're studying is the opening-up of "new possibilities"—how an idea that springs into a subject's head gives birth to new possibilities and creates new routes.

Bringuier: And changes the givens?

Piaget: The givens and everything else. The position of the problems.

Bringuier: But here again the subject may just as well be a child as a scholar?

Piaget: Ah, it's a problem common to the history of science and to intelligence in the process of formation. In the history of science, it's heuristics; for the child, it's the same thing on a small scale . . . Now, we have worked hard, and we have found a good deal more than we first expected to. We feared we hadn't sufficiently limited the subject. In fact, there are enormous differences, depending on the level of the subject.

Bringuier: The level of the child?

Piaget: Yes. But first a word about techniques. The problem was to combine objects, to place cubes on a board in every possible way, or else to indicate all the possible routes between point *A* and point *B*—from a house to a tree. Or, given an object half-hidden in cotton wool, so that you could see only the top, what is below? what are the possibilities? And so forth. Well, what's unbelievable in the little ones of four or five is their lack of mobility and the poverty of the "new possibilities." For instance, they are to make a triangle with three sticks. They make a roof; then they want to close the gap, but the base stick is too short; all they would have to do is change the angle slightly, a displacement of a few millimeters, and they'd have a closed triangle. They want a closed triangle, but they don't have this idea. That's an example. Later, at about seven, the child starts with the base and shows that all triangles—equilateral, isosceles, and scalene—can be built on the same base.

Bringuier: So there's a case of enrichment?

Piaget: Of considerable enrichment. And then, in the half-hidden object, what is below? The little ones suggest something symmetric with what they can see: if what you can see is a triangle, there'll be another triangle below; if it's a half-circle, it will be the other half of the circle, and so forth. But by about age seven they give you possible variations. What's so nice about this is that in nearly all the studies, and we did at least a dozen, all this changes immediately at about eleven or twelve. For example, for the possible routes between *A* and *B,* the little ones give you a straight line, and that's it; later, they try to complicate things, and so forth. As early as about seven, they begin to give you a little set of variations; it can be straight or curved or zigzag. But when they're about eleven . . . I'm thinking of one particular child, whose first remark, when he was asked to show the routes between *A* and *B,* answered, "Why, it's an infinite number. What do you want me to say? It's infinite." And "the infinite" is ordinary from the standpoint of comprehension—that is, as a description or a predicate—and on the other hand, it's limitless from the standpoint of the number of extensions. And so, in every one of the experiments you have an extraordinary evolution according to age level.

Bringuier: When he said "unlimited," he meant . . .

Piaget: I'm the one who said "unlimited"; they say, right out, "It's infinite," or "I can show you as many as you like." And for the dice placed on a board—three dice, three cubes—the child at about age seven says the same thing, "It's infinite; you can put them every way." So then you ask him, "And if the surface were smaller? If, instead of this big square, there were a little square?" he answers, "It's exactly the same thing; but, instead of measuring them in centimeters, you'd measure them in millimeters." The child I mentioned a minute ago added, because he's learning to play the violin, "It's the way it is with the violin. The notes are separated by a certain distance at one end, and they get closer and closer together at the other; but no matter how long the stringboard is, it will always . . ."

Bringuier: It can always be divided.

Piaget: Yes. It will always be an infinity.

Bringuier: And can a parallel be drawn between this, which is the genesis of ideas properly so-called, and the history of science? Since that's one of your pet concerns.

Piaget: Yes, completely. In both cases, the new idea arises from a combination of givens and the context of the problem, on the one hand, and the procedures the subject invents to solve it, on the other. It's the combination of the givens of the problem and the procedures used for solving it. That's the general mechanism. The big question that is raised, particularly for the history of science, is this: Is the possible predetermined in what preceded it, or is it really the creation of something new?" Well . . .

Bringuier: I can guess your answer.

Piaget: Yes, the answer is self-evident. Suppose it were pre-determined. That would mean that there "exists" a set of possibilities already present in the object. But what is the set of possibilities? First of all, it isn't a set—it's highly mobile; each of the possibilities implies others, so you don't know where the set leads. If you speak of the set of all the possibilities, it's anti-nomical, just as is the set of all the sets, because the whole of the possibilities is still only a possibility itself; and what is this whole if it extends indefinitely? Third, in the possibilities, which rest on procedures, you have procedures that are successful, but you also have errors; and of course error comes back into the possibility; the possibility is the set of hypotheses, and some are wrong, some are right. So the errors, if you speak in the language of predetermination . . .

Bringuier: What do you do with them?

Piaget: There was a man who was strictly and admirably logi-cal on this subject, and that was Bertrand Russell. Russell, who was a Platonist when he began his career, considered that all logicomathematical ideas preexist for all eternity in some form and that the subject attains to them outside of himself, by con-cepts, in the same way that he attains the givens of the physical world by perception. So what to do with the erroneous ideas? Well, Russell, who was a great logician, answered: "The errone-ous ideas exist for all time, like the great ideas, in the ragbag of possibilities," and he added, "just as there are white roses and red roses." Now he himself recanted this absurd position, but it shows you the impossibility of this predetermination of pos-sibilities. It's really the opening-up of something new, and it's an opening-up that requires some effort. You see it as a beginner at the age of four or five.

Bringuier: Is this study completed?

Piaget: Yes, it's completed, but it isn't edited. This week the research is being examined in our symposium by guests who have come to offer criticism.

Bringuier: It's going to be the subject of a book?

Piaget: Oh, yes, of course. It's begun. I'll be working on it Sunday, after the symposium ends.

Bringuier: Possibility, as you describe it, must be in the subject's knowledge rather than "predetermined in the object," as you put it?

Piaget: My perspective is this: physical possibility, that is, relative to inanimate objects, exists only in the physicist's head; it's a deductive set, a model into which the individual physicist plunges the real world; and the real world is explicable only in this state, inserted in the set of possible variations, bound together by necessary relations . . .

Bringuier: Of the physicist or the child?

Piaget: Of the physicist; but a fortiori it's the same thing for the child, except for the element of the necessary, which appears only later. But I think that—for example, in D'Alembert's famous Principle of Virtual Work—a system is in equilibrium when the virtual works compensate one another exactly; that is, when the system's possible transformations, as calculated by the physicist, don't occur. If the system is in equilibrium, it's because all the transformations compensate one another, and the algebraic sum is zero. In this case, the virtual work is the physicist's deduction, whereas the object, itself, is in equilibrium; it's static, unmoving. I would say for the physical object, then, that possibility is always relative to the individual interpreting it. On the other hand, biological possibility presents a different problem. Given a genotype or a genetic pool, it contains a series of possible variations that are phenotypes that will arise from interactions between the genotype, the genome, and the environment; and the set of possible variations constitutes what is called "the reaction norm of the genome or the genetic pool," that is, certain variations are compatible with the genetic system, whereas others are incompatible and cannot occur or are not viable. So the notion of the "reaction norm" is the possibility, this time relative to the organism itself. And why do we put possibility into the organism, into the organic object, if we're talking about biology, and confer it on the subject rather than the physical object if we are talking about physics? I would answer that the organism is already a subject; it's the point of departure for the thinking subject . . .

Bringuier: It isn't an object like others . . .

Piaget: No, an organism tends toward goals, it has a teleonomy the physical system doesn't have; and then, too, it uses procedures to attain its goals. And also, when the occasion arises, it's the point of departure for knowledge. From all these points of view, even when there is simply morphological variation, the organism is an active subject using its procedures to realize its goals, its internal teleonomy, which is its conservation, its multiplication, and so on.

Bringuier: And we've come back to one of your basic ideas, which is that there is no break between biology and knowledge?

Piaget: Of course; the source of possibility is in the organism, but its outcome is the logicomathematical disciplines.

Bringuier: So, at the conclusion of this research, since you're coming to the end, does another topic for study seem to be taking shape?

Piaget: Why, certainly. Now we have to study the stages of the necessary. The necessary is always linked with the possible. When you're dealing with a system whose possible variations are deducible and coordinated with one another, you have the relation of necessity among the possibilities. We must study the necessary, which we'll do next season. But when we first began to study possibility, we encountered a phenomenon we might have foreseen; still, we were quite surprised by how widespread it was: it was the initial notion of pseudo-necessity. For instance, children believe that all squares should lie on their bases and that, if you set one of them on its corner, it's no longer a square, it's two triangles—and all kinds of pseudo-necessities like that.

Or, take the child whom I asked, some time ago, "Why does the moon shine only at night and not in the daytime?" He answered, "It's not the moon that decides." So, you see, there's a confusion between the factual and the normative, or between the general law and the necessary law or the necessary relation, which isn't the same thing. Pseudo-necessity is extremely interesting from the point of view of possibility, because, of course, it is a source of limitations. To open up new possibilities is to free oneself from pseudo-necessity and to attain to real variations.

Bringuier: So this is your new field?

Piaget: The new field is the evolution of the necessary.

Bringuier: And afterwards—you don't know yet?

Piaget: I already have my hypothesis: the pseudo-necessary reality at the beginning is a phase during which possible and necessary reality are undifferentiated; then you have differentiation of the three areas; and, finally, reality is absorbed by the two extremes. Every real phenomenon is an actualization from among possibilities. On the other hand, every real phenomenon becomes necessary to the degree to which it is inserted into the system of possible variations, but in necessary relation to them, insofar as it constitutes a deducible model. Consequently, reality becomes both—becomes more or less the point of intersection or interference between the possible and the necessary. That's the hypothesis.

Bringuier: And after that? Can one guess the sequel on hearing this?

Piaget: Well, I suppose we'll have to study either the mechanism of cognitive regulations, eventually, or, perhaps, the idea of reciprocity.

Bringuier: You'll have to make a choice?

Piaget: Well, there are several possible projects. But I'm satisfied to have a program for next year.

Bringuier: Naturally. I was only wondering if you are ever at a loss, at the end of a piece of research, when you find yourself with various studies fanning out ahead of you.

Piaget: Why, yes, of course.

Bringuier: How are you able to decide among them?

Piaget: You can take the easiest one, the simplest one, to begin with. Or the one that actually raises the greatest number of questions from the point of view of our general theories—the one with the most gaps in it.

Bringuier: I may be mistaken, but the approach you have—of conquering successive fields—in a way seems to me to resemble a set of Chinese boxes; the whole of one study, with its result, becomes part of the new field of research.

Piaget: Well, that's our dream. *(Silence.)* They accuse me of . . .

Bringuier: They accuse you of what?

Piaget: The empiricists. Of having a system. They talk all the time about Piaget's "system." I've never had a system. I put successive things together after the fact. I always face the unknown with a new problem and attach the results to those we've already found. Well, of course, that makes a system, but it isn't pre-established with regard to new research. Far from it.

Bringuier: It's a sequential order, like the "stages." You're basically very much a Piagetian. *(Laughter.)*

Piaget: I was less so in the past. But I'm beginning to be, yes.

Epilogue

Piaget has written of his work:

It is my conviction, illusory or otherwise—and the future alone will show which part is truth and which but simple conceited obstinacy—that I have drawn a quite clear general skeleton, but one still full of gaps of such a kind that, in filling them, one will be led to differentiate its connections, in various ways, without at the same time altering the main lines of the system.

The history of the experimental sciences abounds in examples that are instructive in this regard. When one theory succeeds another, the initial impression is that the new one contradicts the old and eliminates it, whereas subsequent research leads to retaining more of it than was foreseen. My secret ambition is that the hypotheses one could oppose to my own will finally be seen not to contradict them but to result from a normal process of differentiation. [*Archives de psychologie,* vol. 44, no. 1 (June 1976).]